EVERY DECISION MATTERS

In Today's World Of Infinite Choices

Written By:

Nicholas J. Matyas

"In a world of endless choices, clarity comes from choosing with honesty and learning to trust yourself as each step unfolds."

- Santiago Dagon

The Discovery Walkabout Collection Of Reflective Writings

Every Decision Matters

In Today's World of Infinite Choices

Santiago Dagon quotations are used with permission from Discovery Walkabout Press, as part of The Discovery Walkabout Collection of Reflective Writings.

This book is a work of reflection. It blends fact and fiction. The names, characters, dialogues, events, and examples are presented for illustrative purposes only. Any resemblance to real persons, living or deceased, is coincidental or used respectfully in service of the story's truth.

Library of Congress Control Number:

Paperback ISBN: 979-8-9936444-3-1

E-Book ISBN: 979-8-9936444-9-3

First Edition 2026

Cover design and layout by Discovery Walkabout Studio

Published by Discovery Walkabout Press

Printed in the United States of America

For permission requests, inquiries, information about educational licensing, collaborations, events, or reprint rights, contact:

Discovery Walkabout Press https://discoverywalkabout.com

PREFACE

A GUIDE TO A DIFFICULT AND CHANGING WORLD

There is a moment in every life when a person stops and quietly wonders how everything became so complicated. It might happen at the kitchen table late at night with bills scattered in front of you. It might happen in the car outside a doctor's office after hearing news that changes the shape of your week or your year. It might happen in the middle of an ordinary Tuesday when you suddenly feel the pressure of being a parent, a partner, a worker, a friend, and a caretaker all at once.

And sometimes it happens for no clear reason at all. You simply pause and think, **Something has shifted. I need a different way of moving through the world**.

I sat across from many people who reached that moment. Some were twenty-two and unsure how to build a life in a digital world that keeps pulling at their attention. Some were forty and tired from holding everyone else together. Some were in their fifties and trying to make peace with choices they believed they should have made long ago. Each person arrived with a different story, but the same quiet question. **How Do I Make Good Decisions in a World That Never Stops Changing?**

This is not an easy world to navigate. You know that already. Information moves faster than the mind can comfortably process. Technology shapes our relationships and our attention. Jobs shift. Economies rise and fall. Families stretch across states and countries. Children grow up in a digital environment that many parents never knew. Parents age while their adult children struggle to balance care, work, and identity.

There is a reason life feels heavy sometimes. You may feel pulled in directions you never expected. You may feel pressure to keep up, to appear fine, to move forward even when you feel unsure of where you are going.

Aristotle once said that knowing yourself is the beginning of wisdom. He lived in a world without screens, without algorithms, without global conflict broadcast into every living room. And yet his words still seem to fit. When life becomes confusing, your inner knowing becomes the map. It may not point to a perfect outcome, but it may help you take the next honest step.

This book is meant to be a companion in that process. A steady voice. A calm one. Not someone who tells you how to live, but someone who walks beside you while you figure out what matters. Decisions are not math problems. They are emotional landscapes. They are shaped by fear, hope, memory, exhaustion, love, regret, culture, and circumstances that shift from one year to another.

Many people believe their decisions are made by logic alone. But life rarely works that way. Most choices begin in a feeling. A hunch. A memory. A small ache that reminds you something is no longer working. Then the mind tries to make sense of what the heart already knows.

In my own work, I have seen how someone may stay in a relationship long after it hurts because the idea of starting over seems unbearable. I have seen how a person keeps saying yes at work even when their body is giving signals that it needs rest. I have seen parents try to raise children while carrying their own unhealed patterns. I have seen adult children care for parents while quietly grieving the loss of who those parents used to be.

These stories do not follow one pattern. But they share one truth. Every decision carries a piece of who you are becoming.

Santiago Dagon once wrote, **"The path of wisdom might be narrow, but your steps do not have to be rushed."** I believe that. Wisdom has a quiet rhythm. It slows you down enough to hear yourself. It invites you to question your habits. It asks you to choose with awareness rather than urgency.

There might be days when your decisions will feel small. What to eat. When to rest. Who to call. When to say nothing. And there might be days when the choices feel life altering. Whether to stay. Whether to leave. Whether to begin something again.

Small or large, each decision has a way of shaping your future self. Not with dramatic force, but with subtle direction. Like a hand on the shoulder guiding you gently toward a different horizon.

As you read this book, I hope you move slowly. Pause when something resonates. Sit with the stories as if you are listening to a friend. Let the ideas breathe. Some sections might feel close to your own life. Others may remind you of someone you love. This is how real understanding begins.

There is an old line from Lao Tzu that says, "A journey of a thousand miles begins with a single step." You have likely heard it before. But the part people forget is that the first step is usually taken with uncertainty. Most journeys begin without confidence. They begin with the willingness to start anyway.

If you take anything from these pages, let it be this. You are allowed to slow down. You are allowed to change your mind. You are allowed to begin again.

Every decision matters. Not because every decision must be perfect. But because every decision reveals what you value, what you believe, and what you hope your life might become.

And that is enough to begin.

CONTENTS

INTRODUCTION

THE DECISION OVERLOAD ERA

There is a particular feeling many people carry these days. A heaviness that does not always announce itself loudly. It shows up in the small moments. Standing in the kitchen trying to decide what to make for dinner after a long day. Staring at a phone screen late at night with too many messages, too many opinions, too many expectations. Sitting in a car before work and feeling something tighten in the chest without any clear reason.

People often say they feel overwhelmed. But overwhelmed does not quite capture it. This is something deeper. Something quieter. A steady pressure that seems to follow many of us from morning until night. And it might be the result of something simple, although not easy. There are too many decisions.

Previous generations had their own struggles. Hard ones. But they did not have to make hundreds of small choices before noon. They did not have to curate their identity every time they opened a screen. They did not have to manage friendships, work relationships, and family communication through a dozen apps. They did not navigate a world where every person with an internet connection could comment on their choices.

You and I live in what might be called the Decision Overload Era. Too much information. Too many paths. Too many loud voices. And not enough quiet space to hear your own.

If you feel exhausted by the simplest tasks, there may be nothing wrong with you. You might simply be living in a world that pulls at your attention in more directions than the human mind was built to hold.

Psychologists sometimes describe this as cognitive fatigue, although the term feels too clinical for what happens inside a real person. It feels more like walking through fog. You can see shapes and possibilities ahead, but nothing feels sharp enough to trust. So you hesitate. Or you rush. Or you freeze.

This is where many of the people I meet begin their work. They say things like, "I do not know what the right choice is." Or, "I feel like every decision might ruin something." Or, "I feel pressure from every side and I do not know who to listen to anymore."

This is not weakness. This is not failure. This is the natural result of living in an environment that demands constant decision-making without offering the emotional space needed to make decisions well.

Aristotle said that excellence is a habit. He was not talking about productivity. He was talking about living with awareness. He believed that a good life is built step by step, choice by choice, with quiet discipline and thoughtful attention. His world was slower. But the principle still applies.

The trouble is that modern life does not pause long enough for most people to hear their own thoughts. There is always another message to answer. Another crisis on the news. Another bill. Another expectation. Another wave of self-comparison after scrolling past someone who appears happier or more successful.

It makes sense that you may feel unsure. It makes sense that you may question yourself. It makes sense that you may feel torn between logic and emotion, or between duty and desire.

Human conversation sounds different when someone finally admits, "I do not know what to do." This is usually when the real work begins. And it often begins with something small.

A breath.

A pause.

A question that feels simple but carries weight. **What Matters Here?**

The truth is that people are not only choosing between Path A and Path B anymore. They are choosing between paths, identities, expectations, online pressures, cultural messages, inherited beliefs, and fears about the future. Every decision sits inside a larger decision. And that can feel paralyzing until you understand it.

This is why clarity has become a survival skill. Not clarity as in certainty. But clarity as in understanding your inner landscape well enough to move with intention.

Santiago Dagon wrote, **"A mind that returns to itself begins to see again."** I have seen this happen. Not dramatically. Not all at once. It happens quietly. A person begins to slow down. A person begins to ask better questions. A person stops looking for perfect answers and starts looking for honest ones.

When someone learns to do that, decisions change shape. They lose some of their heaviness. They stop feeling like traps. They begin to feel like opportunities to move closer to what is true.

The goal of this book is not to remove uncertainty. Uncertainty is part of being alive. The goal is to help you build an inner clarity that holds steady in the middle of a loud and changing world.

Over the next chapters, we will walk through the decisions that shape modern life. Family. Love. Work. Money. Health. Digital habits. Identity. Purpose. And we will do it slowly, with the understanding that real change does not come from force. It comes from awareness.

The Stoic writer Marcus Aurelius reminded himself each morning that his thoughts shape his world. He understood something important. Decision-making is not just about choosing the right option. It is about becoming the kind of person who chooses from a place of inner steadiness.

My hope is that this book helps you touch that steadiness in yourself. Not as a final destination. But as a daily practice. A quiet return to the part of you that already knows the way forward.

This is the beginning of learning how to navigate the Decision Overload Era with clarity, compassion, and a mind that feels like your own again.

PART I

THE INNER WORLD

CHAPTER 1

THE NOISE INSIDE US

1.1 Why Life Feels Louder Than It Ever Did

There is a kind of noise that does not come from the outside at all. It comes from within us. It builds slowly, the way steam collects inside a closed room. You may not notice it at first. You go through your morning routine. You check your phone. You answer a message. You think about work. You think about money. You think about the people who depend on you. You do not pause long enough to see how crowded your mind has become.

And then, one afternoon, you sit down and realize that you have not taken a single deep breath in hours.

Life feels louder now. Not because the world is shouting, although it might be. But because so many parts of your life call for attention at the same time. Work follows you home through your phone. News arrives before you ask for it. Every app invites your opinion. Every decision comes with ten new considerations. The result is a kind of quiet exhaustion that settles in your muscles and your thinking.

People sometimes say, "I feel drained, but I did not do anything unusual today." And I nod because I hear this in my office every week. The truth is that the mind is carrying more than it was built to hold.

There is a line from Marcus Aurelius that says, **"Nowhere can man find a quieter or more untroubled retreat than in his own soul."** He wrote that almost two thousand years ago. He never imagined algorithms. Or constant notifications. Or the subtle pressure to be present everywhere at once. Yet his words still feel necessary.

Because many people no longer know how to reach that inner retreat.

And that is why life feels louder.

It is not simply the world. It is the way the world enters the mind without permission. It fills every corner. It takes up emotional space that you need for yourself. You might feel this in your sleep. You might feel it when you startle easily. You might feel it when you sit in silence and notice that your thoughts do not know how to slow down.

But there is nothing wrong with you. You are reacting to very real pressure. The pressure felt by millions. A pressure that pulls the mind in twenty directions and expects it to function with calm precision.

No wonder so many feel overwhelmed.

1.2 The Emotional Cost of Constant Comparison

Comparison used to happen in smaller circles. A person compared themselves to neighbors. To friends. To coworkers. Now a person compares themselves to the entire world before breakfast.

And the interesting thing is that comparison rarely announces itself outright. It does not always look like envy. It does not always look like insecurity. Sometimes it looks like a faint heaviness. A subtle ache behind the ribs. A feeling that you should be further along, even if you cannot explain why.

You see someone your age buying a home while you struggle with rent. You see someone else raising children and appearing fulfilled. You see someone online celebrating a career victory. And for a moment, your own life feels smaller. Less certain. Less enough.

People tell me, "I know it does not make sense, but I feel behind." And I tell them it does make sense. Because the brain is not built to process the curated lives of thousands of people in one sitting. It reacts emotionally, not logically.

You may know that what you see online is edited. You may know it is filtered. But the emotional system does not care about that. It responds to the image as if it is real. And that response carries weight.

Lao Tzu said, **"When you are content to be simply yourself, and do not compare or compete, everybody will respect you."** This is beautiful. And difficult. Because contentment requires quiet. And the modern world rarely gives it.

Comparison steals joy. But more importantly, it steals clarity. When you compare, you do not see your own life clearly. You see a distorted reflection shaped by someone else's story. And when decisions come from that distorted place, they rarely lead where you hoped.

The emotional cost is subtle but significant. You may lose trust in your own pace. You may rush choices. You may doubt your progress. You may push yourself into exhaustion trying to meet a standard that was never real to begin with.

And honestly, that kind of emotional wear becomes heavy.

1.3 What Happens When Your Mind Never Gets Quiet

A mind that never rests begins to misread signals. It hears threats where there is no threat. It hears urgency in situations that only require patience. It hears failure in moments that are simply human.

When the mind stays busy for too long, you may notice certain signs. You forget simple things. Your patience shortens. Your sleep becomes lighter. Your decisions feel rushed. You might avoid difficult conversations because you fear you cannot handle one more emotional weight.

People sometimes look at me and say, "I feel like I am about to break." But when we talk more, it becomes clear that they are not breaking. They are overloaded.

There is a difference.

The human mind has limits, although those limits are generous. It can hold work stress. It can hold family responsibilities. It can hold long-term worries. It can hold complicated emotions. But not all at the same time, all day, without pause.

Silence is not a luxury. It is medicine. And yet many feel guilty when they sit still. They feel guilty when they rest. They feel guilty when they step away from the noise.

Santiago Dagon once wrote, **"The mind returns to truth only after it remembers how to breathe."** That reflection has stayed with me for years. The mind seeks clarity. It seeks structure. It seeks calm. But it cannot find any of those things in constant motion.

When your mind never gets quiet, your decisions change. They become reactive. They become defensive. They become shaped by fatigue rather than intention.

And fatigue is a poor compass.

The goal is not to become someone who never feels overwhelmed. That is impossible. The goal is to build small pockets of quiet that help you hear yourself again.

1.4 Small Moments That Begin to Steady The Heart

People sometimes expect change to come from big gestures. A long vacation. A major commitment to a new lifestyle. But the truth is that the first real change usually comes from something smaller.

A moment.

A breath.

A pause in the middle of a busy afternoon.

Sometimes it is a decision to sit in your car for one extra minute before walking into work. Sometimes it is choosing to put the phone down during dinner. Sometimes it is saying no to one obligation that no longer feels healthy. Sometimes it is allowing yourself to rest without justification.

These small decisions create emotional space. And emotional space creates steadiness.

Thoreau once wrote, **"It is not what you look at that matters. It is what you see."** When you slow yourself just enough, what you see begins to shift. You notice what your body has been trying to tell you. You notice which relationships support you. You notice which responsibilities are draining life from you. You notice the difference between noise and truth.

And slowly, almost quietly, the heart begins to settle.

You may not feel transformed. That is fine. Transformation rarely arrives with fireworks. It arrives like a soft rearranging of the inner world. One decision. One breath. One moment at a time.

The noise does not disappear. But it loses some of its power. You begin to notice the small, steady voice beneath it. The voice that whispers what you knew all along.

And that is where the next chapter starts.

CHAPTER 2

THE POWER OF SMALL DECISIONS

2.1 The Compound Effect of Daily Choices

There is a belief many people carry that change happens in big moments. The dramatic breakthroughs. The bold decisions. The sweeping promises to finally do life differently. And yes, those moments matter. They mark turning points. They create momentum. But most of the meaningful changes I have witnessed do not begin with a dramatic choice at all. It begins with something small.

A person decides to drink one glass of water before the morning coffee.

A person chooses to walk for ten minutes after dinner.

A person stops checking email before bed.

A person pauses when anger rises rather than speaking too soon.

Small decisions are easy to overlook. They appear insignificant. They feel too simple to matter. But that is the interesting thing. They matter precisely because they are simple. Simple means repeatable. Repeatable means steady. And steady things accumulate.

People often underestimate this. They underestimate the power of one healthy choice made quietly and consistently. They underestimate how the mind shifts when it learns it can depend on itself. They underestimate how life slowly rearranges around small, intentional actions.

Aristotle believed that we become what we repeatedly do. Excellence, he said, is a habit. Not an act. And habits are built one small decision at a time.

You may feel overwhelmed by the larger changes your life seems to require. You may feel unsure how to reshape your health, your relationships, your finances, or your inner world. But the first move is rarely a leap. The first move is usually a step so small you barely feel it.

You do not need to change everything. You need to change one thing at a time. Because one thing becomes two. Then three. And slowly the weight shifts. Slowly you feel more capable, more grounded, more aligned with the person you hope to become.

This is how change accumulates. Quietly.

2.2 When Simple Habits Change the Entire Direction of a Life

A habit is not just a behavior. A habit is a story you tell yourself through action. Each repetition says, "This is who I am.

This is how I move through the world." And when that story changes, everything around it begins to shift.

I have worked with people who transformed their entire emotional landscape through one simple habit. One woman began sitting in silence for three minutes each morning. That was it. Three minutes. With time, those minutes softened her reaction. They helped her see where her stress came from. They reminded her that she could choose how to respond to her day rather than tumble into it.

Another man began writing one honest sentence in a notebook each night. Not a journal entry. Not a full reflection. One sentence. Sometimes it was a fear. Sometimes it was gratitude. Sometimes it was something unresolved. Those single lines helped him understand himself in ways he never had before. They guided decisions he had been avoiding for years.

Simple habits shift identity. They show you something about your own capacity. They prove to you that you can shape the conditions of your life even when the world feels overwhelming.

The mind likes small changes. They do not activate fear. They do not demand sudden reinvention. They feel manageable, which means they last. And when something lasts, it becomes part of you.

Thich Nhat Hanh once said that the present moment is the only moment available to us, and it is the door to all other moments. A habit, when practiced with intention, brings you back into the present moment again and again. And from that moment, new decisions become possible.

Do not underestimate the force of something simple. It may redirect your life more profoundly than anything dramatic ever could.

2.3 Why Tiny Decisions Carry Hidden Emotional Weight

A tiny decision is rarely tiny. Not on the inside. What looks small on the surface often carries meaning beneath it.

You choose to get out of bed when you feel discouraged. That is a decision about hope.

You choose to make a healthy meal instead of ordering whatever is easiest. That is a decision about self-respect.

You choose to send a message to someone you love. That is a decision about connection.

You choose to rest when you feel guilty for slowing down. That is a decision about worth.

Every small choice touches something emotional. Something internal. Something true.

When a person struggles with small decisions, it is rarely because the decision itself is complicated. It is because there is a feeling attached to it. Fear. Shame. Doubt. Fatigue. Old beliefs that whisper things you learned long ago. And when people ignore these emotional undercurrents, they often assume something is wrong with their discipline. But discipline is not the issue. Awareness is.

The mind carries stories from childhood, from culture, from past relationships, from old failures, from inherited expectations.

And these stories influence small decisions without announcing why.

For example, a person may struggle to say no because they fear disappointing others. A person may avoid budgeting because it reminds them of childhood scarcity. A person may resist healthy habits because they associate them with past shame. These emotional roots live beneath the surface. But they shape daily life.

Lao Tzu said, **"The journey of a thousand miles begins with one step."** Everyone remembers this part. But the deeper truth is that the first step is often emotional, not physical. A tiny decision carries the weight of everything that came before it. And when you understand that, you begin to treat yourself with more compassion.

Small decisions are not tests of strength. They are openings. They show where care is needed. They show where old wounds still influence the present. And they show where the next chapter of your life will begin.

2.4 Santiago Dagon Reflection

Santiago Dagon once wrote, **"Every doorway opens one step at a time."** He understood something essential. Life does not ask you to know the entire path. It asks you to take the next honest step. The doorway does not open because you force it. It opens because you approach it with awareness.

One step.

Then another.

Then another.

This is how you enter a new season of your life. You do not arrive with certainty. You arrive with willingness. A willingness to begin. A willingness to choose again. A willingness to trust that small, steady decisions create a future that feels like your own.

So, start where you are. Start with the smallest place that feels possible. Let the step be enough for now. The doorway will open as you walk.

CHAPTER 3

HOW TO THINK BEFORE YOU DECIDE

3.1 Understanding Emotion, Logic, and Intuition

Most people believe they make decisions with logic. They imagine a clean, rational process. Pros on one side. Cons on the other. A clear winner at the end. But real decisions do not work that way. Real decisions involve three forces inside you. Emotion. Logic. Intuition. Each speaks a different language. Each offers something useful. Each carries its own risks.

Emotion speaks first. It is quick. Immediate. It reacts before you even know what happened. A tightness in the chest when a bill arrives. A sense of irritation when someone raises their voice. A drop in your stomach when you sense distance in a relationship. Emotion tells you something important. It tells you how you feel. But it does not always tell you what to do.

Logic arrives later. Slower. More deliberate. It analyzes details. It organizes facts. It builds a case. Logic is essential. It keeps your decisions grounded. But logic can become rigid under stress. It can overthink. It can convince you that safety matters more than truth. Or that certainty matters more than honesty.

Intuition is different. It is quiet. It does not rush. It does not argue. It does not shout to be heard. It feels like a small pull in a certain direction. A sense that something is right for reasons you cannot fully explain. Intuition is not magic. It is a form of internal memory. A collection of past experiences, observations, and emotional patterns gathered over years. The unconscious mind stores more than you realize.

People often ignore intuition because they fear it. They fear choosing without proof. But intuition is not the opposite of logic. It works together with logic. It completes the picture.

Santiago Dagon once wrote, **"Logic clears the path, but intuition chooses the step."** He understood that decision-making is not a battle between inner forces. It is a conversation. A negotiation. A blending of thinking, feeling, and sensing.

When you learn to listen to all three, decisions become clearer. Not perfect. But clearer.

3.2 The Brain Under Stress and Why Decisions Get Cloudy

A stressed brain does not think the same way as a calm brain. This is not a metaphor. This is biology. When stress rises, the body releases chemicals that prepare you to survive, not to reflect. The heart beats faster. Breathing becomes shallow.

Muscles tighten. The logical parts of the brain receive less oxygen. The emotional centers receive more.

This means that stress makes every decision feel larger than it is. Urgent. Heavy. Dangerous. People sometimes say, "I know what I should do, but I cannot seem to do it." And I nod because the problem is not the decision. The problem is the state of the mind attempting to make the decision.

Think of a fogged windshield. The road does not change. The path does not change. The destination does not change. Your clarity changes. Your confidence changes. Your ability to steer safely changes. A stressed brain is like that windshield.

You may notice this when you cannot focus. Or when you replay the same thought again and again. Or when you feel torn between choices that seem equally frightening. Or when you avoid making decisions altogether because the thought of choosing feels overwhelming.

Marcus Aurelius wrote, **"The soul becomes dyed with the color of its thoughts."** He meant that your mental state shapes your perception. Stress colors everything with urgency. Even things that do not require urgency at all.

This is why decisions become cloudy. Not because you do not know how to choose. But because stress narrows your field of vision. It makes the mind rush. It makes the heart fear. It makes the future feel closer than it is.

The solution is not to force clarity. The solution is to steady the mind enough to see again.

3.3 How to Slow Thinking When Everything Feels Urgent

When everything feels urgent, most people speed up. They move quickly. They speak quickly. They act quickly. But urgency rarely requires speed. It usually requires space.

Slowing your thinking begins with one simple truth. You do not need to respond immediately.

You might feel pressure to answer someone right away. Or to reply to a message. Or to make a decision before you are ready. Much of that pressure is emotional, not real. Most situations allow more time than fear suggests.

You can practice slowing your thinking in small ways.

Try this. Next time you feel urgency rising, sit down. Or place your hand on a table. Or touch the back of a chair. Something stable. Something physical. The body grounds the mind. You might take one slow breath. Not dramatic. Just deliberate.

You might tell yourself, "This deserves a moment." That one sentence shifts the internal speed. It signals to the mind that you are choosing awareness rather than panic.

And once the mind slows, choices no longer feel like cliffs. They feel like steps. Manageable. Human. Real.

You can also practice asking simple questions.

What part of me feels pressured? Is this urgency coming from outside or inside? What is the smallest next step?

These questions interrupt emotional momentum. They help the mind step out of fear and into clarity.

Thoreau said, **"The question is not what you look at, but what you see."** Slowing down changes what you see. It widens your options. It softens automatic reactions. It gives the logical and intuitive parts of your mind a chance to join the conversation.

Decisions made in a slower state tend to hold up better. They come from steadiness, not reflex.

3.4 A Therapist's Guide to the "Clarity Pause"

The Clarity Pause is a practice I teach often. It is simple. It is brief. It works. You can use it before making any decision. Large. Small. Personal. Professional. Emotional. Financial.

Here is how it works.

You stop.

You breathe.

You ask three questions.

You answer honestly.

Then you choose.

Not from fear. From awareness.

The three questions are these.

Question One. What Am I Feeling Right Now?

Not what you think. What you feel. Emotion shapes decisions. Naming the emotion weakens its grip.

Question Two. What Matters Most in this Situation?

Not in general. In this moment. Your values become clearer when you ask this directly.

Question Three. What is the Next Honest Step?

Not the perfect step. Not the final step. The next one. The honest one.

This pause might take twenty seconds. Or two minutes. But it creates space. Inside that space, the mind becomes more trustworthy.

People assume clarity requires certainty. It does not. Clarity requires presence. When you are present, you see options you did not notice before. You hear the quieter parts of yourself. You recognize what aligns with your inner truth.

Santiago Dagon once wrote, **"Clarity is the companion of stillness, not certainty."** I have seen this unfold in many lives. The people who learn to pause before they decide start making better choices that feel more aligned. More balanced. More grounded in who they truly are.

Try the Clarity Pause today. Use it on something small. Notice how your body responds. Notice how the decision feels different when you give yourself space.

This is how you begin to think before you decide. Not with pressure. With presence.

CHAPTER 4

THE MIND'S MIRROR

4.1 Anxiety, Depression, and The Wandering Mind

There are days when the mind feels like a room with too many open windows. Thoughts drift in and out without warning. Worries fly across your awareness like leaves in the wind. One moment you feel steady. The next moment you feel unsettled without knowing why. This wandering of thought might not seem like much, but it often carries weight.

Anxiety is not simply worry. Depression is not simply sadness. They are states of mind that shift perception. They tint the world. They change how you hear your own thoughts. They shape your decisions before you realize they have done so.

A person living with anxiety tends to imagine worst outcomes. Not because they believe disaster is certain, but because the mind wants to prepare for pain. A person living with depression tends to minimize their potential. Not because they lack ability, but because the mind has grown tired and cannot envision a hopeful future.

I have heard people say, "I should be stronger than this." Or, "I do not know why I feel this way when nothing bad is happening." And I remind them gently that emotional states do not always respond to logic. Sometimes they arise from patterns deep within the brain. Old stress. Old fear. Old exhaustion.

Marcus Aurelius wrote, **"You have power over your mind, not outside events."** He did not mean that a person can control every thought. He meant that awareness is a kind of strength. When you notice your mental state, you begin to understand your decisions in a different light.

An anxious mind makes choices that seek safety.

A depressed mind makes choices that require the least energy.

A wandering mind makes choices that avoid discomfort.

And none of these choices are failures. They are signals. They show how your inner landscape influences your outer life. The goal is not to silence anxiety or depression overnight. The goal is to understand how these states shape your perception, so you can meet them with compassion rather than judgment.

Santiago Dagon once wrote, **"The mind asks for kindness more than correction."** That line may be the beginning of healing for more people than they realize.

4.2 How Childhood Patterns Influence Adult Decisions

Childhood does not stay in childhood. It follows you. Quietly. Patiently. Sometimes invisible. It influences how you trust. How you love. How you react to stress. How you see yourself in the eyes of others.

A person who grew up in a home where anger arrived without warning might become an adult who avoids conflict at all costs. A person who grew up feeling unseen might become an adult who overworks to prove worthy. A person who experienced abandonment might become an adult who clings to relationships that hurt them. And a person who grew up with emotional instability might become an adult who questions their every choice.

These patterns are not flaws. They are adaptive strategies the child used to survive. The trouble begins when the same strategies continue long after they are needed.

Clients often ask, "Why do I keep making the same mistake." The answer is usually simple, although not easy. The child inside them is still trying to stay safe.

When you begin to recognize old patterns, you gain the power to interrupt them. Awareness creates space. And space creates possibility. You may begin by asking different questions. You may start noticing when your reactions feel larger than the situation. You may feel a shift in the body. A tightening in the stomach. A warmth in the chest. Signals from the past.

Lao Tzu said, **"If you want to know the future, look into your present actions."** Those actions often come from deeper roots. When you understand those roots, you can choose differently. Not perfectly. Not immediately. But honestly.

Childhood does not define you. But it does shape the way you move until you see it clearly enough to choose another path.

4.3 Navigating Self-Doubt and Internal Critics

Self-doubt is one of the most common obstacles I see. It shows up in subtle ways. A hesitation before speaking. A reluctance to try something new. A quiet voice inside that whispers, "You will fail." Or "You are not ready." Or "People will judge you."

Internal critics do not appear out of nowhere. They are built over time. Through past criticism. Through comparisons. Through disappointments. Through moments where you felt small or unseen. The inner critic learns its lines from earlier chapters of your life.

You might think you are the only one who struggles with self-doubt, but I assure you that is not true. Highly successful people feel it. Parents feel it. Young adults feel it. Older adults feel it. Self-doubt does not discriminate. It settles into places where people care deeply about outcomes.

The goal is not to eliminate the critic. The critic will always exist in some form. The goal is to understand its role. That critic tries to protect you. It warns you before you take risks. It reminds you of old pain so you do not repeat it. But protection can become imprisonment if left unexamined.

You can begin speaking to yourself differently.

You can say, "I hear you, but I will think this through."

You can say, "I may not feel ready, but readiness grows with movement."

You can say, "This fear is an echo, not a prediction."

Santiago Dagon once wrote, **"Courage is not the absence of fear, but the decision to walk while fear follows quietly behind."** That reflection holds truth. You do not need to silence doubt. You need to walk with it at a pace that honors your growth.

Self-doubt softens when you begin treating yourself with the same compassion you offer others. And that shift changes everything.

4.4 The Role of Therapy, Community, and Mindfulness

Healing rarely happens in isolation. Change rarely happens without support. The mind is a complex landscape, and no one should be expected to navigate it alone.

Therapy offers a space where you can speak without fear of judgment. A space where your inner world is taken seriously. A space where old patterns can be examined gently. Many people believe therapy is for crisis only. But therapy is also for growth. For clarity. For guidance. For understanding your emotional foundation.

Community matters in a similar way. A healthy community does not solve your problems. It steadies you while you solve them yourself. It gives you perspective. It gives you encouragement. It reminds you that you are not meant to carry everything alone.

Mindfulness ties these together. It teaches you how to sit with yourself. How to observe your own mind without immediately reacting to it. Mindfulness is not about achieving perfect calm.

It is about noticing. Your thoughts. Your sensations. Your emotions. Your patterns.

Marcus Aurelius practiced something similar. He reflected each evening. He reviewed his day. He looked for places where he reacted without awareness. His writing shows a man who understood that clarity grows through observation.

Therapy provides the tools.

Community provides the support.

Mindfulness provides the awareness.

Together, they create an environment where better decisions become possible.

4.5 Wisdom from Marcus Aurelius and Lao Tzu

Ancient wisdom remains because it speaks to something timeless in us. Something human. Something unchanged by technology, culture, or circumstance.

Marcus Aurelius often reminded himself, **"You have power over your mind, not outside events. Realize this, and you will find strength."** He understood that what we nurture internally quietly guides how we live externally. When you pause to notice your thoughts, you are not just observing the present moment. You are shaping the direction of what comes next.

Lao Tzu offered a quieter reflection. **"Nature does not hurry, yet everything is accomplished."** He invites us to remember that growth has its own pace. Decisions have their own seasons. Life unfolds in ways that cannot be forced.

Santiago Dagon echoes these voices in his own way. **"The mind becomes clearer each time you return to yourself."** He reminds us that clarity is not found outside. It is found in the quiet moments when you allow yourself to see honestly.

These teachings do not offer rules. They offer direction. Gentle direction. Human direction. They point toward awareness, patience, and self-understanding. And these qualities strengthen every decision you will ever make.

This chapter ends where the next begins. With the understanding that you can change your relationship with your own mind. And once that relationship changes, life begins to open in ways you may not have imagined yet.

PART II

THE LIFE YOU ARE BUILDING

CHAPTER 5

MONEY, SECURITY, AND THE FEAR OF FALLING BEHIND

5.1 Inflation, Bills, and The Weight Of Financial Uncertainty

There is a particular silence that settles over people when money becomes uncertain. It is the kind of silence that happens when you are sitting alone at the table, looking at a bill you were not expecting. Or when you check your bank account and feel that familiar drop in your stomach. A sense of heaviness that spreads through the chest. A worry that feels old, even if your life is new.

Inflation does something subtle to the human mind. It creates a tension between what you believe you should be able to afford and what you actually can. And that gap carries emotional weight. It can make people question their competence. Their value. Their future. Even when none of this is a personal failure.

You might feel frustrated that groceries cost more. That rent rises faster than wages. That medical expenses seem to multiply. You might feel embarrassed when you cannot keep up with friends who appear stable. You might feel shame when you decline an outing because you are trying to stretch what you have.

Financial stress is not just about numbers. It is about identity. It is about safety. It is about wanting to give your children a better life while wondering how you will manage your own. It is about waking up and trying again even when the long-term picture seems blurry.

Marcus Aurelius once wrote, **"Do what you can, with the tools you have, in the place you stand."** He understood something important. No one can control the rise and fall of economies. But a person can choose how they move within them. One choice at a time.

You are not weak for feeling overwhelmed. You are human in a world that is shifting faster than many people can adjust. The weight you feel is real. The courage it takes to carry it is real as well.

5.2 Housing Dilemmas: Rent, Buy, Stay, Move`

Housing decisions strike a deep part of the heart. A home is not just a structure. It is a symbol. A feeling. A place where you want to exhale. A place where you want to belong. A place that should feel safe. Which is why these decisions feel so heavy.

Should you rent because buying a house feels impossible? Should you buy because renting feels unstable? Should you stay in a city you love but cannot afford? Should you move somewhere more practical but less emotionally fulfilling? Should you live closer to your parents? Or further from old stress? Or closer to your children's school? Or near the job that pays well but drains your spirit?

Housing dilemmas contain more than financial questions. They contain emotional ones. They reveal what you believe about comfort, success, independence, family connection, and long-term dreams.

One client once told me, "I feel embarrassed that I am still renting at my age." When we explored the feeling, it became clear that the embarrassment did not come from the number on the lease. It came from an old belief that adulthood equals ownership. A belief passed down from parents who lived in a different economy, at a different time, with different prices, different pressures.

Housing decisions today carry complexity that previous generations did not face. Wages have not kept up with costs. Cities have become crowded. The price of stability has increased. And yet the emotional expectations remain.

Before making a housing decision, pause and ask yourself: What do I need right now?

Not ten years from now. Not what society tells me I should want. Now.

Lao Tzu wrote, **"To attain knowledge, add things every day. To attain wisdom, remove things every day."** Housing decisions often require exactly that. Removing the noise. Removing the pressure. Removing the imagined voices of others. Until you hear your own. A home should hold your life, not your fear.

5.3 Caring for Children While Caring for Aging Parents

There is a unique kind of exhaustion that comes from standing in the middle of two generations. Children who need you for growth. Parents who need you for stability. And you, somewhere in the middle, trying to stay whole while everyone around you leans in your direction.

This middle place might feel overwhelming. You may feel guilty for not doing enough for your parents. You may feel guilty for not being fully available to your children. You may feel guilty for not having the energy you think you should have. But guilt does not tell the truth. Guilt tells the story you fear most. And that story is rarely accurate.

I have spoken with many people who whisper, "I feel alone in this." And I remind them that more people than they know live in this same emotional space. They wake early to get children ready for school. They stay up late to call a parent who is struggling. They squeeze errands into lunch breaks. They worry about the future of two generations at once while trying to hold themselves steady. It is a lot.

Your decisions carry emotional layers. If you choose to help your parents more, you may worry if you are neglecting your children. If you choose to focus on your children, you may fear your parents will feel abandoned. These are not decisions of convenience. These are decisions of the heart.

The truth is that caring for others requires caring for yourself. Not as a luxury. As a foundation. If you burn out, everything collapses around you. Your compassion fades. Your patience thins. Your health suffers.

Santiago Dagon once wrote, **"The one who carries others must remember to rest."** And that reflection might be the most important decision-making principle for anyone in this stage of life. You may not always find balance. But you can find rhythm. And rhythm is enough.

5.4 How Money Shapes Identity and Self-Worth

Money is not just currency. It is meaning. It is history. It is emotional. It is tangled into childhood messages, cultural expectations, old wounds, and personal dreams. It shapes identity in ways people rarely recognize.

If you grew up with scarcity, you might feel a constant fear of losing what you have, even when your life is stable. If you grew up around wealth, you might feel a quiet pressure to match it, even if your values or opportunities differ. If you grew up hearing arguments about money, you might feel anxious every time finances come up in a relationship.

Money carries stories. Stories about success. Stories about failure. Stories about worth.

I hear people say, "I should be further along." Or "I feel embarrassed about my financial situation." Or "I do not want anyone to know I am struggling." And I ask them gently, "Who taught you that your value is tied to your account balance?" Because someone did. Somewhere along the way. Often without meaning harm.

Money becomes emotional because people believe it defines them. But money is not identity. Money is a tool. A necessary tool, yes. But still a tool. A person's character cannot be measured in dollars. A person's worth cannot be measured in assets. A person's humanity cannot be measured in financial milestones reached or missed.

Marcus Aurelius said, **"Very little is needed to make a happy life. It is all within yourself.**" He understood that inner strength holds more weight than financial fortune. Money may influence your choices. But it does not define your value.

5.5 How to Make Decisions When Everything Feels Risky

When life feels unstable, every decision feels like a gamble. You may hesitate to change jobs because the economy feels uncertain. You may hesitate to move because the cost scares you. You may hesitate to invest, start something new, leave something old, or speak a truth you have avoided because risk feels larger than courage.

Here is the part most people forget. Every decision involves risk. Even the choice to stay where you are.

The goal is not to live without risk. The goal is to understand which risks align with your values, and which risks drain your life. Risk becomes manageable when it is connected to meaning.

When you face a difficult decision, ask yourself three things.

Will this choice bring me closer to who I hope to become?

Will this choice support the stability I need right now?

Will this choice honor my emotional and financial limits?

You do not need to know the entire future. You need to understand the direction that feels honest.

Sometimes the best choice is the safest. Sometimes the best choice is the boldest. Sometimes the best choice is the one that allows you to breathe again.

Santiago Dagon wrote, "**The future does not ask for certainty, only sincerity.**" When you choose with sincerity, even risky decisions carry a sense of peace. A sense that you acted from awareness, not fear.

Life will always contain risk. But you are not fragile. You are capable. You have survived difficult seasons already. You have made decisions that shaped your path. You will make more. And each one matters.

CHAPTER 6

DIGITAL LIFE AND SOCIAL OVERLOAD

6.1 Technology Addiction and Shrinking Attention

There is a moment each day when many people reach for their phones without thinking. The hand moves before the mind notices. It might happen in bed before the first light enters the room. It might happen at the dinner table while waiting for food to cool. It might happen in the middle of a conversation without meaning disrespect. It is almost automatic now. As natural as breathing. And yet, it shapes your inner world in ways that often go unseen.

Technology addiction rarely appears dramatic. It appears subtle. A small pull in the mind. A restless desire to check something. Anything. A fear of missing out on news or messages. A sense that silence must be filled. That boredom must be avoided. That pauses must be used for stimulation rather than reflection.

People often tell me, "I feel distracted all the time." Or "I cannot stay focused anymore." Or "My mind jumps from one thing to another and I do not know how to stop it." And I remind them gently that their mind is responding to an environment designed to capture attention.

Technology companies study human behavior. They design features that reward the brain with small hits of pleasure. Small bursts of novelty. Patterns that keep you coming back. There is nothing wrong with you for responding to this. You are responding exactly the way a human brain responds to reward.

But there is a cost. A shrinking attention span. A sense of mental clutter. A feeling that life moves faster than you can process. And the cost does not reveal itself only in your mind. It reveals itself in your decisions. Because a distracted mind makes shallow choices. It reacts quickly but without depth. It loses the ability to sit with a question long enough for intuition to answer.

Marcus Aurelius cautioned himself, **"A mind disturbed by passions is like a battlefield after war."** In a digital world, the mind is rarely allowed to rest. It is pulled in every direction by noise, alerts, and endless information. Over time, the inner life grows agitated. Fatigued. Crowded with too much input and too little space to breathe. And honestly, this quiet weariness may be one of the defining struggles of our time.

6.2 When Scrolling Replaces Living

There is a difference between watching life and living it. A difference between observing others and experiencing yourself.

And yet, many people spend hours each day scrolling through the moments of others while their own moments pass unnoticed.

Scrolling replaces living when it becomes a reflex. A filler for every gap. Every pause. Every difficult feeling. A person may scroll to escape stress. Or to avoid loneliness. Or to silence a thought they do not want to face. And the more they scroll, the more disconnected they may feel.

I once worked with someone who said, "I scroll at night because it makes me feel less alone, but then I end the night feeling emptier than when I started." That statement is more common than people admit.

Scrolling gives the illusion of connection. But it does not give the nourishment of connection. It shows glimpses of other lives. Not the full truth. Just the curated fragments. The bright parts. The beautiful parts. The impressive parts. A highlight reel that feels real enough to trigger comparison, but incomplete enough to leave you unsatisfied.

Look, it is fine to enjoy your phone. It is fine to laugh at videos. It is fine to catch up on people you care about. But when the digital world becomes the primary source of stimulation, the inner world begins to weaken.

Life may begin to feel less vivid. Less textured. Less grounded in the senses. Food tastes duller when eaten in front of a screen. Conversations feel thinner when attention is divided. Walks lose their beauty when every quiet moment is interrupted.

Lao Tzu observed, **"To the mind that is still, the whole universe surrenders."** When scrolling replaces living, stillness disappears. The mind rushes from one moment to the next, consuming everything yet absorbing very little. Time feels busy, but fulfillment feels distant. A real life, it turns out, does not come from more input. It comes from learning how to be fully present where you already are.

6.3 Real Connection in an Online World

Connection has always been essential to human well-being. But now, connection takes many forms. Text messages. Video calls. Social media comments. Group chats. These can be helpful. They allow people to bridge distance. They allow friendships to continue across time zones. They allow families to stay involved in each other's lives.

But digital connection is different from embodied connection. The body communicates in ways that cannot be captured through a screen. Tone of voice. Small gestures. The pause before someone shares something personal. The softening of the face when someone feels seen. These moments shape trust. They build closeness. They create safety.

In a digital world, relationships can feel both plentiful and shallow. A person may have hundreds of contacts but feel profoundly alone. Real connection requires vulnerability. Attention. Warmth. And these qualities require time. They require presence. They require something digital life cannot fully replicate.

People sometimes tell me, "I feel connected to everyone, but close to no one." And that statement reveals something important. Connection is not measured by quantity. It is measured by depth.

Santiago Dagon once wrote, **"The heart does not open to noise. It opens to attention."** This is true in friendships. In partnerships. In families. If you want deeper relationships, you may need to create deeper attention. You may need to choose conversations over commentary. Presence over performance. Listening over scrolling.

Digital life is a tool. Real connection is a need.

6.4 What to Do When You No Longer Trust Your Own Judgment

One of the consequences of living in a world filled with advice, opinions, experts, influencers, and algorithms is that people begin to doubt their own judgment. When every decision comes with a dozen conflicting viewpoints, uncertainty grows. When every choice is examined publicly or compared privately, confidence weakens.

A person may ask themselves, "Do I really know what I want?" Or "Is my intuition reliable?" Or "Why do others seem so sure when I feel unsure?" And over time, this doubt erodes something essential. Self-trust.

When you no longer trust your judgment, decisions become heavier. You hesitate more. You rely too heavily on others. You look for perfect answers in imperfect places. You may even outsource your choices to people who do not understand your life.

The way back begins with something simple. You practice trusting yourself again. In small steps. Without demanding perfection.

You start by noticing which decisions felt right, even when you are unsure. You recall times in the past when your intuition guided you well. You observe the difference in your body when something aligns compared to when it does not.

You also limit the number of voices influencing you. Not everyone deserves access to your decision-making process. Not everyone has earned the right to shape your direction. This includes well-meaning friends. And charismatic online personalities. And strangers whose opinions carry the weight you should be giving only to yourself.

Marcus Aurelius advised, **"Look well into yourself. There is a source of strength that is always ready to spring up if you will look."** He understood that clarity is not something you chase outward. It is something you cultivate inward. Self-trust returns slowly. But it returns.

6.5 Choosing Healthier Digital Habits One Decision at a Time

Healthy digital habits do not require a dramatic reset. They require small decisions. A moment of awareness before reaching for the phone. A decision to leave it in another room during dinner. A decision to remove apps that drain your energy. A decision to set boundaries with the digital world the same way you set boundaries with people.

You can start small.

Turn off one notification.

Create one hour each night without screens.

Take one walk without your phone.

Eat one meal with full presence.

These decisions build clarity. They create mental spaciousness. They deepen emotional resilience. They remind the mind that it belongs to you, not to your devices.

And slowly, something shifts. You begin to feel less reactive. Less hurried. Less consumed by the highlight reels of others. More attuned to your own life. More aware of your needs. More present with your family, your relationships, your work, your inner world.

Santiago Dagon wrote, **"What you give your attention to becomes your home."** If your attention goes to noise, your inner life becomes noisy. If your attention goes to presence, your inner life becomes steady.

Digital habits shape mental health. Emotional clarity. Decision-making. Relationships. Identity. And you have the power to choose each habit one decision at a time.

In this chapter, you learned how digital life shapes the mind. In the next, you will learn how relationships shape the heart.

CHAPTER 7

LOVE, FAMILY, AND THE TIES THAT SHAPE US

7.1 Dating in a World of Illusions and Endless Options

Dating has always carried its challenges. Nervousness. Uncertainty. Hope. Vulnerability. But today, dating sits inside a digital world that reshapes the entire emotional landscape. Endless profiles. Countless choices. Highlighted lives. Curated personalities. And the quiet pressure to appear impressive rather than real.

People often tell me, "I do not know who is genuine anymore." Or "I feel like everyone has one foot in and one foot out." And I understand why. The modern dating environment encourages constant evaluation. Swipe left. Swipe right. Keep options open. Keep guard up. Wait for something better. And this creates an illusion of abundance, but not the experience of connection.

When everything is a possibility, nothing feels certain. When attraction is based on curated images, chemistry becomes harder to trust. When people fear vulnerability, relationships struggle to deepen.

Marcus Aurelius once wrote, **"If someone does wrong, it is because he knows no better."** Many people in the dating world are not acting from malice. They are acting from fear. Fear of choosing wrong. Fear of missing out. Fear of showing their true selves.

Love requires courage. And courage is difficult when the world teaches people to protect themselves at all costs.

If you are dating, remember something simple. Look for character, not performance. Look for consistency, not intensity. Look for someone who shows up in small ways. Someone whose presence feels steady. Someone who chooses you even when no one is watching. You deserve something real. Even in a world built on illusion.

7.2 Recognizing Unhealthy Attachment

Unhealthy attachment does not always look dramatic. It can appear subtle. Slow. Emotional. It might look like waiting anxiously for someone to text you back. Or bending your needs to avoid conflict. Or feeling responsible for someone's moods. Or staying in a relationship because leaving feels unbearable even when the relationship has become painful.

People often misunderstand attachment. They assume that strong attachment means strong love. But attachment and love are not the same. Attachment is about emotional survival. Love is about emotional expansion.

A person with unhealthy attachment may feel drawn to relationships that trigger old wounds. They may feel safest in situations that feel familiar, even if familiar means unstable.

Lao Tzu offered a reflection that fits here. **"When I let go of what I am, I become what I might be."** Unhealthy attachment holds you inside the version of yourself shaped by the past. Healthy attachment helps you grow into the person you are becoming.

Signs of unhealthy attachment often include:

You fear abandonment even in stable moments.

You silence your needs to keep peace.

You feel responsible for your partner's emotions.

You stay in relationships that shrink you.

You confuse intensity with intimacy.

Recognizing these patterns is not failure. It is awakening. Awareness is the first step toward healing. And healing changes the way you choose relationships for the rest of your life.

Santiago Dagon once wrote, **"Love that harms the self is not love. It is memory."** And that reflection may gently guide you away from what hurts and toward what heals.

7.3 The Emotional Cost of Divorce and Co-Parenting

Divorce carries a weight that many people do not talk about honestly. It is not simply a legal process. It is an emotional unraveling. A dismantling of routines, memories, expectations, and identity. Even when divorce is necessary, the heart experiences loss.

People often carry guilt. They worry about their children. They wonder if they tried enough. They question their judgment. They feel grief for the version of life they hoped for. All of this is normal. Divorce is not a clean break. It is a complicated transition. One that requires time and gentleness.

Co-parenting adds another layer. You may need to communicate with someone you no longer trust. You may need to coordinate schedules while managing your own emotional recovery. You may feel overwhelmed by the responsibility of protecting your children from adult conflict.

I have heard people say, "I feel like I am failing my kids." And I remind them that children do not need perfect parents. They need consistent ones. They need parents who show up. Who listens. Who apologizes when necessary. Who creates stability even when the family structure has shifted.

Thoreau wrote, **"Things do not change. We change."** Divorce does not determine the future of your family. Your choices after divorce do. Your emotional presence does. Your willingness to heal does. Divorce may change the shape of your life. But it does not diminish the depth of your love.

7.4 Raising Children in a Digital World

Raising children today requires navigating challenges no previous generation faced. Technology is woven into every part of a child's life. Education. Friendship. Entertainment. Identity. And parents often feel conflicted. They want to protect their children. But they do not want to isolate them. They want to limit screens. But they do not want their children to fall behind socially. They want to teach independence. But they fear the dangers of the online world.

Many parents tell me, "I feel lost. I do not know the right approach." And that honesty is important. Parenting in a digital world requires flexibility, awareness, and intentionality. Not perfection.

Children are shaped by what they see. If they see parents overwhelmed by devices, they learn that constant distraction is normal. If they see parents choosing presence, they learn that presence matters.

Healthy digital parenting involves:

Setting boundaries that support emotional regulation.

Explaining why limits exist.

Teaching children how to recognize digital influence.

Modeling healthy habits yourself.

Balancing technology with real-world experiences.

Children do not need a screen-free life. They need a balanced life. One where imagination, outdoor play, conversation, boredom, and creativity coexist with digital tools.

Santiago Dagon wrote, **"Children learn the rhythm of life from the rhythm of their parents."** Your presence shapes their presence. Your habits shape their habits. Your decisions become their foundation.

7.5 When Parents Age and Roles Reverse

There is a moment many adults quietly dread. The moment when a parent begins to decline. When strength becomes fragile. When memory fades. When independence shifts into dependence. And the child becomes the caretaker.

This reversal of roles carries deep emotion. Grief. Frustration. Compassion. Confusion. A sense of responsibility that feels enormous. A longing for the parent who once guided you. A fear of losing them entirely.

People often say, "I feel guilty no matter what I do." And I understand. Caring for aging parents requires constant decision-making. Medical choices. Financial choices. Safety decisions. Living arrangements. And none of them feel simple.

Old wounds may resurface. Old dynamics may return. Families may disagree on what is best. And beneath it all lies the emotional truth that you are witnessing the fading of someone central to your life.

Lao Tzu reminds us, **"Those who care deeply suffer deeply."** Suffering is not a sign you are doing something wrong. It is a sign you are human. And you care.

The goal is not to carry everything alone. The goal is to build a network of support. Siblings. Friends. Professionals.

Community resources. You deserve help. And your parents deserve care rooted in love, not burnout.

Caring for parents is hard. But it can also be meaningful. A chance to offer the kindness they once offered you. A chance to heal old misunderstandings. A chance to honor the fullness of their life.

7.6 Boundaries Without Guilt

Boundaries are not walls. They are doors. They allow what is healthy to enter and prevent what is harmful from staying. But many people struggle deeply with boundaries. They fear disappointing others. They fear conflict. They fear being misunderstood.

Some believe that saying No is unkind. But saying Yes to everything is not kindness. It is self-erasure.

Healthy boundaries sound like:

I care about you, but I cannot take that on right now.

I need time to think before I commit.

I want to help, but I must protect my own well-being too.

I can listen, but I cannot solve this for you.

These statements are not selfish. They are responsible. They prevent resentment. They create emotional clarity. They allow relationships to grow in healthier ways.

Marcus Aurelius said, **"The happiness of your life depends on the quality of your thoughts."** Boundaries protect those thoughts. They create the space you need to think clearly. To rest. To choose intentionally.

Santiago Dagon wrote, **"A boundary is a promise to yourself."** That might be the simplest and most accurate truth. Boundaries are not about controlling others. They are about respecting yourself.

This chapter has explored the ties that shape your life. In the next, we will look at work, purpose, and the quiet weight of burnout.

CHAPTER 8

WORK, PURPOSE, AND THE BURNOUT GENERATION

8.1 Choosing Work in a World That Never Stops Changing

Work once carried clearer pathways. A job led to a career. A career led to stability. Stability led to retirement. That rhythm shaped the identity of earlier generations. But the world has shifted. Industries rise and fall. Job descriptions evolve. Companies restructure. Entire fields transform overnight. What felt stable a decade ago may feel uncertain today.

People often tell me, "I do not know what to do next." Or "My career feels like sand slipping through my fingers." And I understand why. Work today requires not only skill, but adaptability. Not only effort, but emotional resilience.

Choosing work in this environment can feel intimidating. You may ask yourself whether you should stay somewhere safe. Or take a risk on something new. You may wonder if passion matters more than income. You may question whether your job aligns with your values. These questions are not indulgent. They are essential. Work takes up a large portion of your time, your energy, and your identity. It shapes your sense of belonging. It influences your mental health.

Marcus Aurelius advised, **"Occupy yourself with few things, but do them well."** In a world of endless options, this wisdom matters. You do not need to do everything. You need to choose work that aligns with your strengths and your season of life.

Work is not only a job. It is part of the story you are writing. Choose with intention. Choose with awareness. Choose with the understanding that your worth is not measured by productivity, but by presence.

8.2 The Role of Meaning in Career Satisfaction

There is a difference between a job and a calling. And there is a space in between where many people reside. A job provides income. A calling provides fulfillment. Many people hope for both, but life does not always align neatly. It is possible to work in a job you tolerate while creating meaning outside of it. It is possible to love your work and still feel tired. It is possible to build purpose slowly, piece by piece, without knowing what the final picture will become.

Meaning does not always come from grand achievements. It often comes from small contributions. A moment of kindness to a coworker. A task completed with care. A project that challenges you to grow. A sense that your work makes life a little better for someone.

People sometimes tell me, "My job feels empty." And I ask them what part of their job feels aligned with who they are? Often, there is at least one thread. One part that still feels real. A mentor relationship. A creative aspect. A chance to help. When that thread is nurtured, meaning grows.

Meaning also grows when you allow yourself to be present. When you slow down enough to notice what you are contributing. When you remember that your work is not only about results, but the person you become as you do it.

Lao Tzu taught, **"Do the difficult things while they are easy, and do the great things while they are small."** He reminds us that direction unfolds over time, not in a single moment of revelation. Many people wait for certainty before they move. But clarity is usually born through movement. Through trying, adjusting, and paying attention to the quiet signals within. You begin to notice what steadies you and what weighs you down. Meaning is not something that suddenly appears. It is something you tend, patiently, as it grows.

8.3 How AI Reshapes Job Security

Artificial intelligence has introduced a new kind of uncertainty into the workforce. People worry about being replaced. They worry about losing relevance. They worry about falling behind the rapid pace of technological change. These worries are understandable. Technology shifts the landscape faster than most people can comfortably adjust.

But here is something important. AI does not replace human qualities. It replaces tasks. It replaces repetition. It replaces what does not require emotional intelligence or human insight.

The skills that endure are deeply human. Creativity. Empathy. Critical thinking. Emotional presence. Moral judgment. Relationship building. These qualities cannot be automated.

People often ask me, "Should I be worried?" And I tell them that worry is natural, but paralysis is not necessary. The goal in this new era is not fear. The goal is adaptability. Curiosity. Willingness to learn. Willingness to evolve. The ability to blend human strengths with technological tools.

AI is often misunderstood, as if it arrived outside the long arc of human progress. In reality, it belongs to the same evolutionary pattern that has guided innovation since the beginning of time. Humans have always created new tools to extend their abilities, to work more clearly, and to make life a little better. AI is simply the latest expression of that impulse. At its best, it functions as a general-purpose tool that strengthens what already exists and opens new ways of working. It does not replace human creativity. It supports it. AI excels at organizing, optimizing, and learning from what is already known. Humans remain the ones who ask the deeper "what if" questions, and who imagine possibilities that do not yet have a name.

Marcus Aurelius said, **"What stands in the way becomes the way."** If AI changes your field, it may also reveal new possibilities. New roles. New paths. New ways to use your gifts. Do not underestimate your humanity. It is your advantage.

8.4 When Burnout Becomes a Turning Point

Burnout does not arrive suddenly. It builds slowly. A heavy feeling in the morning. A lack of energy that sleep does not fix. A sense of emotional numbness where passion once lived. A shrinking of patience. An ache in the body that lingers. A mind that feels foggy. A heart that feels distant from itself.

People often ignore these signs because they believe burnout means weakness. It does not. Burnout means you have been strong for too long without rest. Burnout means your body is asking you to stop before something inside breaks.

I once worked with someone who said, "I do not feel anything anymore." That was not depression. It was emotional depletion. A survival response after years of pushing beyond healthy limits.

Burnout is not the end of your path. It is a turning point. It is your mind and body telling you that something must change. Your workload. Your boundaries. Your expectations. Your environment. Your self-compassion.

Santiago Dagon wrote, **"Exhaustion is not a sign of failure. It is an invitation to return to yourself."** And that invitation might be the beginning of a new season. One built on healthier rhythms. One that honors your limits. One that restores your sense of direction. Burnout asks you to reconsider the life you are choosing. And that reconsideration is powerful.

8.5 Decisions That Restore Purpose

Purpose is not something you discover once and keep forever. Purpose evolves. It shifts with age. With experience. With loss. With parenthood. With changing priorities. Many people feel ashamed when their purpose changes, as if they are betraying their earlier dreams. But purpose is meant to grow with you.

Restoring purpose begins with listening. Listening to the part of you that feels alive when certain activities fill your day. Listening to the part of you that feels drained when something no longer fits. Listening to the subtle desires that whisper beneath the noise.

Here are decisions that often restore purpose:

Choosing work that aligns with your values rather than your image.

Choosing rest before your body collapses.

Choosing boundaries that protect your energy.

Choosing projects that challenge you.

Choosing people who support your growth.

Choosing to learn something new.

Choosing to let go of what no longer serves you.

Meaning grows from these choices. One honest decision at a time.

Thoreau wrote, **"Go confidently in the direction of your dreams. Live the life you have imagined."** He spoke of confidence not as bold certainty, but as steady intention. The willingness to take small steps toward a life that feels true.

Purpose is not found in achievement. Purpose is found in alignment. And alignment begins the moment you choose to live in a way that honors your inner world as much as your outer demands.

This chapter closes with the reminder that your work matters. Not because of what you produce, but because of who you become through it. In the next chapter, we explore the world around you and how external forces shape your emotional landscape and your decisions.

PART III

THE WORLD AROUND YOU

CHAPTER 9

LIVING IN TIMES OF UPHEAVAL

9.1 Political Tension and Compassion Fatigue

There is a weight many people carry these days, although they rarely name it directly. It is the exhaustion that settles into your mind and heart when you open the news. It is the heaviness that lingers after conversations about the state of the world. It is the quiet ache you feel when people you care about begin to argue about things neither side fully understands.

This weight is called Compassion Fatigue. It happens when the world asks you to care about everything all at once. Wars. Elections. Injustice. Division. Economic instability. People in pain. Systems breaking. And on top of that, the demands of your personal life. Your job. Your children. Your parents. Your health.

A human heart can hold a great deal. But it was not built to hold the entire planet's grief every day.

Political tensions add a layer of emotional pressure. People speak with certainty about complex issues. Families get divided. Friendships become strained. Social media amplifies outrage and anger. And this constant exposure to conflict drains your capacity for empathy.

People often tell me, "I feel numb. I know I should care, but I cannot process anymore." And I remind them that numbness is not indifference. It is self-protection. The mind shuts down when it has reached its emotional limit.

Marcus Aurelius wrote, **"If it is not right, do not do it. If it is not true, do not say it."** That simple guidance holds power during times of upheaval. You do not need to take on every issue. You do not need to hold every opinion. You do not need to fight every battle. You need to protect your compassion. Not scatter it until nothing remains.

9.2 Climate Anxiety and The Global Future

Climate anxiety has become a quiet companion for many people. You sense it when summer heat becomes stronger than before. You sense it when storms feel more violent. You sense it when you hear about oceans rising or forests burning. A subtle fear about the future. A concern for your children. A worry about the world they will inherit.

This anxiety is not irrational. It is emotional realism. It is the mind responding to real changes in the world. But climate anxiety becomes harmful when it paralyzes rather than activates. When it makes you feel powerless. When it convinces you that nothing you do matters.

Lao Tzu said, **"You accomplish the great by attending to the small."** Climate action is the same. No individual can fix the entire planet. But each person can influence the world within reach. Their home. Their habits. Their community. Their choices.

Santiago Dagon wrote, **"Hope grows when action becomes personal."** Climate decisions become meaningful not when they solve everything, but when they align with your values. Small steps. Repeated. Thoughtfully. Without frenzy.

Anxiety does not need to disappear for you to act. You can carry concern in one hand and courage in the other.

9.3 Making Grounded Choices When the World Feels Unstable

Unstable times create unstable emotions. When the world feels unpredictable, people often feel pressure to make big decisions quickly. Move. Save. Spend. Divorce. Quit. Escape. Start over. Drastic action sometimes feels like the only way to regain control. But urgency can distort clarity.

When the world becomes chaotic, the most grounded decisions come from slowing down rather than speeding up. Asking simple questions. Listening to the body. Feeling the difference between fear and intuition. Distinguishing between impulse and insight.

People tell me, "I cannot think clearly anymore." And I explain that clarity is not something you wait for. It is something you build. Through small steps.

You can ask yourself:

What is within my control?

What is not mine to carry?

What matters most in this particular moment?

What decision will protect my long-term well-being?

Marcus Aurelius encouraged returning to inner stability during external storms. **"You have power over your mind, not outside events. Realize this, and you will find strength."** He understood that a person can remain steady even when the world is not.

Your decisions do not need to be perfect. They need to be grounded. And grounding requires presence.

9.4 The Danger of Extreme Voices

Extreme voices are loud because fear is loud. Outrage is loud. Anger is loud. Suffering is loud. The dark side is loud. And the digital world rewards loudness.t amplifies the most dramatic opinions. It pushes people toward polarized thinking. It presents lies with the same confidence as truth.

This environment makes it difficult to distinguish wisdom from manipulation. Many people feel overwhelmed by conflicting information. They feel pulled toward charismatic figures even when something feels off. They feel trapped in echo chambers without realizing they have entered one.

Extreme voices often simplify complex issues. They offer easy answers. They promise certainty. They create enemies. They demand loyalty. These voices comfort the anxious mind for a moment, but they weaken independent thinking over time.

Lao Tzu wrote, **"The wise man is one who knows what he does not know."** Extreme voices claim to know everything. That is the warning sign.

You will find clarity by stepping back. By avoiding sources that stir anxiety more than understanding. By choosing information that educates rather than inflames. By remembering that truth does not shout. Truth speaks steadily.

Santiago Dagon wrote, **"Noise divides. Quiet reveals."** When you move away from the extremes, you hear your own guidance more clearly.

9.5 Who to Listen to When Everyone Is Shouting Advice

In a world full of advice, the hardest part is deciding which voice deserves trust. Friends offer opinions based on their experiences. Strangers online speak with confidence based on partial information. Professionals give guidance shaped by their field. Influencers speak with passion shaped by financial incentive or personal agenda. Even family members speak from their own fears and hopes. So how do you choose.

Begin with this.

Listen to people who help you think, not people who tell you what to think.

Trust voices that encourage reflection rather than obedience.

Trust voices that offer perspective, not panic.

Trust voices that ask questions, not demand conclusions.

Trust voices that understand nuance, not oversimplification.

Trust voices that align with your values, not your fears.

Marcus Aurelius advised, **"The opinion of ten thousand men is of no value if none of them knows anything about the subject."** Quantity does not equal quality. Volume does not equal truth.

You can also trust your body. Notice how you feel when hearing someone's guidance. Tight. Anxious. Pressured. Confused. That is usually a sign to step back. Calm. Clear. Balanced. Open. That is usually a sign that the advice aligns with your deeper wisdom.

Santiago Dagon said, **"Seek the voice that steadies you, not the one that excites you."** Excitement can mislead. Stillness clarifies.

You are allowed to create distance from overwhelming opinions. You are allowed to choose whose influence shapes your life. You are allowed to decide whose voice deserves your attention.

This chapter explored how the outer world affects your inner world. The next chapter turns inward again, toward meaning, presence, and the spiritual compass that guides your decisions.

CHAPTER 10

SPIRITUALITY FOR A RATIONAL MIND

10.1 Seeking Meaning Without Dogma

There comes a time in many lives when the mind begins to wonder about meaning. Not always in dramatic ways. Sometimes it begins with a quiet question. Why am I here? What am I meant to learn? How should I live in a world that feels uncertain? These questions do not require religious belief. They arise from the human heart itself.

Spirituality, in its simplest form, is the search for meaning. Not dogma. Not strict doctrine. Not rigid systems. Spirituality is the gentle movement toward understanding your place in the larger story of life.

People often say, "I am not religious, but I feel something deeper." And I understand. A rational mind does not need to choose between logic and wonder. The two can coexist. Reason explains the world. Meaning deepens it. Science tells us how life works. Spirituality asks why life moves us in the ways it does.

A person can seek meaning through nature. Through art. Through service. Through silence. Through relationships. Through self-awareness. Meaning arrives in many forms, and each one is valid.

Thoreau wrote, **"The question is not what you look at, but what you see."** Meaning does not appear when the world changes. It appears when perception deepens. When you slow down. When you listen inwardly. When you become curious again.

Santiago Dagon once wrote, **"Truth is not a place you reach. It is a place you return to."** Meaning is not a final destination. It is a rhythm. A practice. A gentle unfolding.

10.2 Stillness as an Inner Compass

Stillness is not the absence of noise. It is the intentional pause within it. A moment when the mind settles long enough for the deeper voice within you to speak. That voice is not dramatic. It is not loud. It is often felt rather than heard.

Stillness is where intuition becomes clear. Where emotions soften. Where thoughts lose their frantic momentum. Where the mind remembers that it does not need to run in every direction.

People often tell me, "I do not know how to quiet my mind." And I remind them that stillness is not about forcing silence. It is about creating space. A small moment where you no longer chase distractions. A breath taken slowly. A step taken consciously. A moment when you sit without reaching for a screen.

Stillness is the doorway to clarity.

You might experience it when watching a sunset. Or when sitting by a window in early morning light. Or when walking through a familiar neighborhood. Or when holding a warm cup in your hands. These moments remind you that clarity is not created. It is uncovered.

Gandhi said, **"In the midst of darkness, light persists."** Stillness is where that light becomes visible again. It is not mystical. It is practical. It steadies the nervous system. It opens the mind. It aligns the heart. It helps you recognize the difference between a decision made from fear and a decision made from truth.

Stillness is not a luxury. It is a compass.

10.3 Wisdom from Thoreau, MLK Jr., and Gandhi

Ancient teachings often feel timeless because the human heart has not changed as much as the world around it. Even in a fast, digital age, wisdom from long ago speaks with surprising clarity.

Thoreau encouraged intentional living. **"Go confidently in the direction of your dreams. Live the life you have imagined."** He understood that life becomes meaningful when you choose your direction with awareness rather than drift through it without intention.

Martin Luther King Jr. taught courage of conscience. **"Faith is taking the first step even when you do not see the whole staircase."** He reminded us that certainty is not required for movement. Courage begins with one honest step.

Gandhi grounded spirituality in compassion. **"The best way to find yourself is to lose yourself in the service of others."** He recognized that meaning deepens when you contribute to the lives around you, not when you isolate yourself from them.

These teachings align with what many people seek today. A spirituality rooted in compassion. In service. In presence. In integrity. Not dogma. Not division. Not fear.

Santiago Dagon echoes this same thread when he writes, **"Your inner light grows each time you act in harmony with your values."** It is a reminder that meaning is not found in grand philosophies. It is found in daily choices. In honesty. In kindness. In steadiness.

Wisdom is not meant to overwhelm you. It is meant to guide you gently.

10.4 Practices That Bring Clarity Back to The Self

Spiritual clarity is not mysterious. It is practical. It begins with small habits that quiet the mind and bring you back to yourself.

You do not need rituals that feel foreign. You do not need complex beliefs. You do not need elaborate routines. You need moments that reconnect you to your inner world.

Here are practices that help:

Sit in silence for one minute.

Not meditation. Just sitting. Feel your breath. Notice your thoughts without chasing them.

Take a slow walk without your phone.

Let the world move around you. Notice sounds. Colors. The weight of your steps. These small details bring you into presence.

Write one honest sentence each day.

Not a journal entry. One sentence. Something you feel. Something you hope. Something you fear. This single act builds emotional awareness.

Ask yourself one grounding question.

What do I need right now? Not tomorrow. Not next month. Now.

Practice gratitude quietly.

Not as a performance. As an internal acknowledgment of something that brings warmth to your life.

Notice your reactions without judging them.

Every reaction teaches you something. About your fears. Your desires. Your boundaries. Your inner truth.

Spirituality is not a separate part of life. It is woven into every decision. Every breath. Every relationship. Every moment of awareness.

Santiago Dagon wrote, **"Clarity is a home you build one quiet moment at a time."** That reflection holds the heart of this chapter. Meaning does not need to be sought far away. It begins where you are. It begins with the willingness to return to yourself.

In the next chapter, we explore what happens when life breaks, how regret shapes our choices, and why second chances often arrive after the heart has softened.

CHAPTER 11

FAILURE, REGRET, AND THE POWER TO BEGIN AGAIN

11.1 How Regret Shapes the Decisions Ahead

Regret is one of the most powerful human emotions. It stays quiet at first. A small memory. A brief sting. A wish that something had unfolded differently. But over time, regret can grow heavier. It can shape how you see yourself. How you trust yourself. How you choose your future.

Many people believe regret is a sign of failure. But regret is simply a sign of awareness. The mind is looking backward because something inside you knows you could have acted differently. The fact that you recognize it means you have grown.

Regret can shape decisions in two ways. It can make you fearful. Or it can make you wiser.

Fear makes you avoid risk. Avoid love. Avoid truth. Avoid movement. Fear whispers, "Do not try again. You will only repeat the past." That voice feels protective, but it is a cage.

Wisdom uses regret differently. Wisdom asks, "What did this teach me?" And then chooses differently going forward. Regret becomes a turning point. A moment of clarity.

Thoreau wrote, **"Never look back unless you are planning to go that way."** The past exists to inform the present, not imprison it.

Regret shapes your future when you allow yourself to learn from it without punishing yourself for being human.

11.2 When Life Breaks… And What Comes After

There are experiences that change a person permanently. A love that ends suddenly. A job that collapses. A friendship that fractures. A dream that falls apart. A loss that reshapes the landscape of your life.

People often say, "I feel broken." And I sit with them. Quietly. Because brokenness is not something to rush. It is a real emotional state. It deserves gentleness.

When life breaks, something inside you cracks open. The part that believed everything was predictable. The part that believed you had more time. The part that believed certain people or roles would last forever.

This breaking is painful. But it is also honest. It reveals what truly matters. It shows which parts of your life were fragile. It shows which relationships were held together by habit rather than love. It shows what you have been avoiding. It shows the truth beneath the surface.

After the breaking occurs, something else happens. Slowly. Not immediately. Not cleanly. You begin to rebuild. You begin to see a new version of yourself forming. One that carries scars, yes. But also carries wisdom. Patience. Strength you did not know you possessed.

Gandhi said, "**Strength does not come from physical capacity. It comes from an indomitable will.**" You may not feel strong while breaking. But you are learning a strength that only lived beneath the surface until life forced it upward.

Breaking is not the end of the story. It is the middle. The part where transformation begins.

11.3 A Therapist's Perspective on Emotional Repair

Emotional Repair is not about forgetting. It is about integrating. It is about understanding what hurts you, how it shaped you, and how you can live forward without reenacting old wounds.

When people come to life coaching after disappointment or heartbreak, they often ask, "How do I move on?" And I tell them that healing begins when you stop trying to erase the past and start learning from it. Healing is a process of relief, reflection, and renewal.

Relief comes first. The moment you give yourself permission to stop pretending you are fine. The moment you allow tears. The moment you admit that something mattered to you deeply.

Without this relief, the body stays braced. The heart stays armored.

Reflection follows. Quietly. You begin to see patterns. You notice where you ignored your intuition. Where you overextended yourself. Where you stayed too long. Or left too soon. These reflections are not meant to punish. They are meant to reveal.

Renewal arrives last. Not as a sudden brightness, but as a small shift. You begin to trust yourself again. You begin to imagine new possibilities. You begin to feel life return in small forms. A moment of laughter. A sense of curiosity. A desire to try again.

Marcus Aurelius reminded himself, **"The impediment to action advances action. What stands in the way becomes the way."** Emotional repair follows this same quiet logic. What hurts draws our attention. What breaks asks to be understood. The wound begins to teach. The loss opens a passage. And the difficulty, slowly and often unwillingly, becomes the very force that moves us forward.

Healing does not erase what happened. It transforms your relationship to it.

11.4 Santiago Dagon Reflection

Santiago Dagon once wrote, "Every ending knows the way back to beginning." It is a gentle reminder that life moves in cycles. What appears final often becomes a new start. What feels lost often becomes insight. What breaks often becomes space for something truer.

Endings are not failures. Endings are transitions. They lead you toward new clarity. New courage. New identity. New direction.

An ending teaches you how to release. A beginning teaches you how to trust again. And the space between the two teaches you how to listen inwardly.

If you are facing an ending, remember this. You have not reached the conclusion of your story. You have reached a chapter that will one day make sense in ways you cannot yet see.

The beginning is already forming. Quietly. Patiently. Deep within you. And when you are ready, life will open again.

PART IV

LIVING WITH AWARENESS

CHAPTER 12

TIME, MORTALITY, AND WHAT TRULY MATTERS

12.1 The Shock of Realizing Life Is Finite

There is a moment in adulthood that changes everything. It might happen suddenly after a diagnosis in your health. It might arrive quietly while attending a funeral. It might surface during a conversation with your child. Or with your aging parent. A moment when the mind fully understands something it always knew but never felt.

Life is Finite.

For years, people move through life with a kind of unconscious belief that time stretches endlessly ahead. There will be time to repair a relationship. Time to start a dream. Time to take better care of the body. Time to apologize. Time to rest. Time to love more honestly.

But then something happens. And the truth arrives. There is not endless time. There is only the time that remains.

This realization can feel like a shock. A tightening in the chest. A sense of urgency mixed with sadness. A sudden clarity about what matters and what does not.

People often tell me, "I did not realize how quickly life moves." And I tell them that this awareness is not meant to frighten. It is meant to awaken. Mortality is not the enemy. It is the teacher. It encourages presence. It encourages honesty. It encourages kindness. It encourages intentional decisions rather than accidental living.

Marcus Aurelius wrote, **"Do not act as if you had ten thousand years to throw away."** He understood that urgency can be harmful when born of anxiety, but powerful when born of truth.

When you accept that time is precious, you begin to live differently. You choose differently. You love differently. You forgive differently. You rest differently. You stop waiting for life to begin. You begin it now.

12.2 Gratitude as a Moment-By-Moment Decision

Gratitude is often misunderstood. People imagine it as something grand. Something that appears after major blessings. Something associated with celebrations or happy seasons. But gratitude is smaller than that. More ordinary. More practical.

Gratitude is a decision. Moment by moment. A quiet recognition of what is still good even in difficult times.

You feel it when you drink warm coffee on a tired morning.

You feel it when your child laughs at something small.

You feel it when a friend sends a message at the right moment.

You feel it when you step into sunlight after a long day indoors.

These moments appear simple. But they anchor you. They widen your perspective. They soften anxiety. They bring attention back to the present where life actually happens.

People sometimes worry that gratitude means ignoring pain. It does not. Gratitude is not denial. Gratitude is awareness. Pain may exist. But so does beauty. Regret may exist. But so does possibility. Fear may exist. But so does breath.

Gandhi said, **"There is more to life than increasing its speed."** Gratitude slows the world long enough for you to see the details you have overlooked.

Gratitude is a constant awareness of what is already present, not a reaction to what is missing. A Persian proverb from the thirteenth century, often attributed to Sa'di, speaks to this truth: **"I cried when I had no shoes, but I stopped crying when I saw a man without feet."** It is a quiet reminder that blessings rarely vanish. More often, they fade from view when our attention narrows to what we lack. Gratitude gently widens that view again.

When practiced intentionally, gratitude becomes a form of clarity. You begin to understand what nourishes you. You begin to understand what drains you. You begin to understand what you want more of and what you are ready to release.

Gratitude changes decision-making. It strengthens the part of you that can see truth without distortion.

12.3 Slowing Down Enough to Notice What Is Real

The pace of modern life encourages rushing. Rushing through work. Rushing through meals. Rushing through conversations. Rushing toward the next task without experiencing the one in front of you.

Slowing down is a radical act.

Slowing down does not mean doing less. It means doing things with presence. It means noticing small details. The sound of someone's voice. The warmth of water on your hands. The way your breath shifts during stress. The expression on your partner's face when they are tired. The whisper of intuition beneath the noise.

When you slow down, the real world becomes visible again. Not the digital world. Not the imagined future. The Real One.

I once spoke with a woman overwhelmed by life. Work. Children. Bills. Worries. She said, "Everything feels like a blur." And I asked her to describe one moment from her morning. Just one. She paused. She realized she could not remember any details. The entire morning had been consumed by rushing.

She began practicing short pauses. A moment before opening her laptop. A moment before leaving the car. A moment before speaking when frustrated. These pauses did not slow her productivity. They slowed her mind. And slowing her mind changed her experience of the day.

Scripture reminds us in **Book of Proverbs**, **"Better one handful with tranquility than two handfuls with toil and chasing after the wind."** Slowing down does not mean giving up progress. It means releasing unnecessary strain. The rush eases.

The mind clears. Decisions feel more grounded. And the heart, no longer pushed beyond its limits, finds room to rest and respond with greater openness.

Slowness is not inefficiency. Slowness is awareness.

12.4 Lessons from Aging Parents and Dying Friends

Aging parents teach a person more about time than any book ever could. Their fading strength. Their slower steps. Their forgetfulness. Their stories told again and again. Each moment reminds you that nothing remains unchanged. That life moves in one direction. That love becomes more tender as dependency grows.

Many people feel conflicted caring for parents. They feel sadness. They feel frustration. They feel guilt. They feel gratitude. All at once. This mixture is normal. Love at the end of life is rarely simple. It is layered in feelings and emotions. Soft in some places. Heavy in others.

When a parent begins to need you in ways they never did before, you begin to see your own life differently. You notice how quickly decades pass. You notice how precious conversations become. You notice the importance of small gestures. A warm meal. A ride to an appointment. A patient tone. A moment of forgiveness.

Dying friends teach similar lessons. They remind you that relationships matter more than achievement. That laughter matters more than resentment. That presence matters more than perfection. People rarely discuss regrets about money or status at the end of life. They speak about time. Time wasted. Time misunderstood. Time taken for granted.

Thoreau said, **"Our truest life is when we are in dreams awake."** Awareness of mortality awakens this truth. It brings clarity. It removes what is unimportant. It highlights what is essential.

Santiago Dagon wrote, **"When you understand that life is brief, every moment becomes a doorway to meaning."** Mortality is not meant to terrify. It is meant to prioritize. It is meant to help you choose the kind of life that feels honest. Loving. Kind. Present.

This chapter invites you to see time not as an enemy but as a guide. A reminder that every decision carries weight because every moment carries meaning.

In the next chapter, we explore leadership, legacy, and the quiet responsibility of becoming the mentor you once needed.

CHAPTER 13

BECOMING THE MENTOR YOU ONCE NEEDED

13.1 Leadership Without Titles

Leadership is often misunderstood. Many people imagine leaders as those with titles, authority, or influence. But true leadership rarely begins there. True leadership begins quietly. Internally. In the way you live. The way you speak. The way you carry your values through ordinary moments.

Leadership is not a position. It is presence.

You lead when you choose patience in a moment of frustration.

You lead when you tell the truth even when the truth feels difficult.

You lead when you listen fully to someone who feels unseen.

You lead when you make a decision that reflects integrity rather than convenience.

Every person influences the world around them. Through tone. Through behavior. Through example. This influence happens whether you intend it or not. Leadership becomes powerful when you choose to use that influence with care.

People sometimes tell me, "I am not a leader." And I remind them that someone is always watching them. A child. A sibling. A coworker. A friend. A partner. A younger version of themselves held inside their own memory. You may not realize how many people take cues from your behavior.

Marcus Aurelius wrote, **"Waste no more time arguing what a good man should be. Be one."** Leadership lives in this simple principle. You become the example rather than debate it. You embody the values you hope others will practice.

You lead without needing recognition. You lead without needing applause. You lead because it is the person you have chosen to be.

13.2 Teaching Through Example

People learn far more from your actions than from your advice. Children notice how you treat others. Employees sense whether you respect them. Friends watch how you respond to stress. Partners study your tone. Younger people study your choices. Even strangers observe your small gestures.

Example shapes character more powerfully than instruction.

If you want your children to be kind, let them see you apologize when you make a mistake.

If you want your partner to trust you, let them see consistency in your words and actions.

If you want your team at work to feel safe, let them see you stay calm under pressure.

If you want your family to communicate honestly, speak truthfully yourself.

Example creates safety. It builds trust. It inspires growth.

Thoreau said, **"Goodness is the only investment that never fails."** When you live with goodness, you become a quiet teacher. Your presence becomes a guide. People begin to ask you questions. They begin to share their struggles with you. They begin to trust your judgment, not because you claim to know everything, but because you demonstrate steadiness.

Santiago Dagon wrote, **"The world changes one person at a time, beginning with the one you become."** Your example is your influence. Your example is your legacy.

Teaching through example is not about perfection. It is about sincerity. When others see you try, learn, adjust, and grow, they feel permission to do the same.

13.3 Healing Generational Wounds

Every family carries wounds. Some are spoken. Some are unspoken. Some are passed down through stories. Some live in silence. Patterns repeat. Hurt echoes. Beliefs and fears move from one generation to the next until someone finally says, "This will not continue with me."

Healing generational wounds is one of the greatest acts of leadership a person can offer.

It looks like choosing gentleness where there was once anger.

It looks like choosing boundaries where there was once chaos.

It looks like choosing truth where there was once secrecy.

It looks like choosing patience where there was once shame.

It looks like choosing presence in a family that once lived at emotional distance.

People often tell me, "I do not want to become like my parents." And I remind them that rejecting unhealthy patterns is not enough. Healing requires replacing those patterns with healthier ones. Breaking cycles. Creating new ways of relating. Offering the compassion you wish had been offered to you.

Healing does not require blaming anyone. Earlier generations carried their own wounds. Their own fears. Their own limitations. Understanding this softens the heart. You begin to see your parents as human, not as symbols of perfection or failure.

Gandhi said, **"The weak can never forgive. Forgiveness is the attribute of the strong."** Strength is not anger. Strength is the ability to hold pain with compassion while choosing a more loving path forward.

Santiago Dagon wrote, **"The wound stops with the one who chooses awareness."** Awareness is the beginning of healing. And healing is the beginning of generational change.

13.4 Living A Life Someone Else Can Trust

When people reflect on someone they admire, they often use the same words. Steady. Honest. Kind. Reliable. Present. Not perfect. Human. Someone they could trust.

Living a life someone else can trust means aligning your actions with your values. It means speaking truth even when it is uncomfortable. It means showing up consistently. It means honoring your commitments. It means treating others with dignity. It means being gentle with yourself so you can be gentle with others.

Trustworthy living is not about impressing people. It is about contributing something good to the world through the way you move within it.

You become someone others trust when:

Your words match your actions.

Your temper does not control your relationships.

Your compassion outweighs your ego.

Your presence feels safe rather than unpredictable.

Your guidance comes from care, not control.

Leadership is not about being followed. It is about being worthy of being followed if someone chooses to. And you become worthy through the quiet decisions you make each day.

Marcus Aurelius wrote, **"Do not be wise in words. Be wise in deeds."** One act of integrity speaks louder than a thousand opinions.

Santiago Dagon once wrote, **"Be the person your younger self wished to meet."** That reflection captures the heart of this chapter. You cannot change the mentors you lacked. But you can become the mentor who changes someone else's life.

Leadership begins within you. It grows through example. It becomes healing. And eventually, it becomes legacy.

This chapter closes the journey of awareness. The epilogue opens the doorway to what comes next: the courage to keep choosing with intention in a world that asks for your attention every day.

CHAPTER 14

WHAT WOULD SANTIAGO DAGON DO?

A Collection of Wisdom for Everyday Decisions

There are moments in every life when clarity fades. Moments when the heart pulls in one direction while the mind pulls in another. Moments when fear complicates simple choices. Moments when decisions feel heavier than they should. In these moments, people often ask for guidance, not because they lack intelligence, but because they long for steadiness. They long for a voice that speaks calmly, with compassion, with a depth that does not rush.

That is the essence of the question: **What would Santiago Dagon do?**

Santiago is not a figure of perfection. He is a figure of awareness. He pauses. He listens. He honors intuition without denying logic.

He examines fear without surrendering to it. He considers the emotional cost of a choice as carefully as the practical one. He believes that the right decision is rarely the one that feels easiest, but the one that feels most honest.

Santiago would begin every decision with stillness.

He would breathe before thinking.

He would slow the heart before weighing options.

He would let the mind settle long enough for truth to rise.

He would explore the pros and cons, not as a list, but as a dialogue between heart and mind. The mind asks, "What makes sense?" The heart asks, "What feels true?" Santiago honors both, knowing that wisdom lives in the space where they meet.

Below are ten everyday scenarios, and how Santiago Dagon might approach each one.

Scenario 1 - Should I Stay in a Job That Drains Me But Pays Well.

Santiago would sit quietly with the question. He would ask the body first, not the brain. Does the body tense when imagining staying? Does it soften when imagining leaving? He would then examine the emotional cost. The tired mornings. The rising irritability. The numbness.

He would acknowledge the practical realities. Bills. Responsibilities. Stability. But he would also ask, "What is the long-term price of staying here?"

He would likely say, "Begin with one small step toward a healthier future. You do not need to quit today. You need to start choosing yourself again."

The best decision would appear slowly. Through honesty, not panic.

Scenario 2 - Should I End a Relationship That Feels Uncertain.

Santiago would not rush. He would explore whether the uncertainty comes from fear or from truth. Fear blurs clarity. Truth sharpens it.

He would ask, "Does this relationship expand you or shrink you?"

He would listen to the tone in your voice.

He would listen to the pauses between your words.

He would remind you that endings are not failures. They are transitions. If the relationship is harming the heart, he would encourage release. If the relationship is challenging old wounds, he would encourage inner reflection before acting.

The decision comes from understanding your needs, not avoiding discomfort.

Scenario 3 - Should I Relocate to a New City for Better Opportunities.

Santiago would consider both longing and loss. He would ask, "What are you moving toward?" and "What are you moving away from?" He would help you separate excitement from escape.

He would acknowledge fear. Moving changes identity in ways people rarely expect. But he would remind you that growth often requires new soil.

He would say softly, "Choose the place where your life feels possible."

The answer would arise when your values become clear.

Scenario 4 - Should I Confront a Friend Who Has Hurt Me.

Santiago would pause. He would ask about your intention. Are you seeking revenge? Or clarity? Or healing? He would help you understand the emotional cost of silence. Resentment grows in unspoken spaces.

He would encourage compassion without self-abandonment. He would say, "Speak the truth kindly. Boundaries are not punishment. They are guidance."

He would remind you that friendship built on honesty becomes stronger, even after difficult conversations.

Scenario 5 - Should I Invest Money During Uncertain Economic Times.

Santiago would acknowledge both prudence and possibility. He would examine your fears. He would explore your stability. He would help you identify what level of risk aligns with your emotional and financial capacity.

He would say, "Do not invest from fear. Invest from intention." He would guide you to choose steady steps over impulsive ones.

The decision would come from grounded awareness rather than trend or pressure.

Scenario 6 - Should I Cut Back on Technology Even If It Feels Uncomfortable.

Santiago would ask, "What do you lose when you are always connected? And what do you gain when you disconnect?" He would help you see that discomfort often signals dependence, not necessity.

He would remind you that stillness strengthens intuition. He would say, "Protect your attention. It is the doorway to your inner world."

The decision would not be about deprivation but about reclaiming presence.

Scenario 7 - Should I Pursue a Dream That Feels Unrealistic.

Santiago would smile softly. He would ask, "Does this dream come from the heart or from ego?" He would help you explore your deepest motivations. He would remind you that dreams evolve, and that growth does not require applause.

He would say, "Take one small step. Dreams are built the same way truth is built. Slowly."

He would guide you to pursue the dream without sacrificing stability or self-care, balancing courage with wisdom.

Scenario 8 - Should I Forgive Someone Who Has Apologized but Still Worries Me.

Santiago would look directly into your hesitation. He would ask whether forgiveness is being confused with trust. Forgiveness is an internal release. Trust is earned through consistent behavior.

He would gently say, "Forgive if it brings peace. Trust only if the other person has become trustworthy."

Forgiveness frees you. Trust protects you. Santiago honors both.

Scenario 9 - Should I Care for an Aging Parent Even If It Disrupts My Life.

Santiago would acknowledge the emotional conflict. Love, duty, grief, frustration, and fear. He would not romanticize the hardship. He would ask what support exists. He would explore whether your decision preserves both compassion and sustainability.

He would say, "Care for them, but do not lose yourself in the process." He would guide you toward shared responsibility rather than self-sacrifice.

The best decision honors both generations.

Scenario 10 - Should I Change My Life After Realizing I Am Not The Person I Hoped To Be.

Santiago would breathe with you. He would place no judgment on your past. He would remind you that identity is not fixed. He would say, "Awareness is the beginning of becoming."

He would encourage small, meaningful shifts rather than dramatic reinvention. He would remind you that becoming yourself is a lifelong practice.

And he would say quietly, "The person you hope to be is not far away. That person is growing inside you right now."

Santiago Dagon's Approach Is Not Mysterious. It Is Mindful. Compassionate. Steady.

He listens inwardly.

He honors intuition.

He respects logic.

He acknowledges fear without letting fear decide.

He chooses from values, not from pressure.

His wisdom can become your wisdom when you pause long enough to hear yourself. Because the question, **"What would Santiago Dagon do?"** is really an invitation to ask: **"What would my most honest, grounded, compassionate self do?"** And that self already knows the way.

EPILOGUE

The Courage to Decide Again

There is a quiet truth that sits beneath every chapter of this book. A truth that people often overlook when their lives become complicated and heavy. The truth is this. You are allowed to decide again. You are allowed to choose differently. You are allowed to begin from where you stand, not from where you wish you had been.

Life rarely unfolds in straight lines. It twists. It surprises. It breaks in places you thought were solid. It opens in places you believed were closed. And because of this, decisions made years ago may not fit the person you have become today. That is not failure. That is growth.

People often tell me, "I wish I had known then what I know now." And I understand. Awareness arrives on its own schedule. You learned what you learned at the time you were ready. And when life teaches you something new, you earn the right to choose again.

Every decision shapes your direction. But no decision locks your future. Not permanently. Not conclusively. You might have chosen a job that drained you. You might have stayed in a relationship that hurt you. You might have neglected your health. You might have avoided a dream out of fear. You might have spoken words you regret. You might have stayed silent when honesty was needed.

And still, you can choose again.

Marcus Aurelius wrote, **"The impediment to action advances action."** What stands in your way becomes your path. Obstacles become turning points. Mistakes become teachers. Regret becomes clarity. Pain becomes insight. You do not move on from the past. You move forward with it. And your next decision becomes part of that movement.

Santiago Dagon once wrote, **"Life offers new doors the moment you are willing to knock."** That reflection has accompanied many people through difficult transitions. Because it reminds them that opportunities do not disappear. They shift. They wait. They return when you are ready to approach them with a steadier heart.

Choosing again requires courage. Not loud courage. Quiet courage. The kind that whispers, "I am allowed to grow." The kind that says, "I will try once more." The kind that does not wait for perfect conditions or absolute certainty. The kind that accepts the possibility of imperfection and moves anyway.

The courage to decide again appears in small ways.

You decide to rest when exhaustion has felt normal for too long.

You decide to speak kindly to yourself after years of self-criticism.

You decide to reach out to someone you love.

You decide to let go of something that has taken more than it has given.

You decide to pursue something that brings meaning.

You decide to forgive someone, even if that someone is yourself.

Life does not require bravery at every moment. It requires bravery at certain moments. The moments when you stand at a crossroads and feel the familiar pull of your old patterns. The moments when you know the comfortable path and the honest path are two different roads. The moments when you are tired of repeating the same story and want to live a new one.

In those moments, you have a choice. Not a perfect one. A human one.

Choose slowly. Choose gently. Choose with awareness. And when the choice becomes difficult, pause until you feel yourself again.

Søren Kierkegaard, a Danish philosopher, theologian, and writer often regarded as the "father of existentialism." wrote, **"Life can only be understood backwards, but it must be lived forwards."** He reminds us that forward movement does not require perfect certainty. You are allowed to begin, pause, and begin again. What matters is that the step you take belongs to the life you are actually living now, not the one you think you should have figured out by this point.

This book does not end with certainty. It ends with possibility. You have learned how your mind works. How your emotions shape your decisions. How your relationships influence your path. How the world presses in on your inner life. How purpose shifts. How meaning grows. How endings become beginnings.

Now, you carry that awareness with you.

You will face new choices. Some easy. Some painful. Some confusing. Some liberating. And each one will invite you into a deeper understanding of who you are and who you hope to become.

You do not need to know your entire future. You need only the courage for the next decision.

And you already have it.

The courage to decide again lives within you. It always has.

APPENDICES

APPENDIX A

THE DECISION MAKER'S TOOLKIT

Every person needs a set of tools they can return to during moments of uncertainty. Tools that calm the mind. Tools that steady the heart. Tools that bring clarity back into view when life feels overwhelming or confusing.

The following practices are simple. They do not require specialized training. They do not require perfect discipline. They require only willingness. A willingness to pause, reflect, and choose with awareness rather than impulse.

These tools are not rigid formulas. They are companions. Gentle guides. You can adapt them. You can use them daily or only when life becomes heavy. Their purpose is to bring you closer to yourself, not to give you answers from outside.

Santiago Dagon once wrote, "**A wise decision begins in stillness.**" The tools below are designed to help you reach that stillness, even briefly, so you can hear your own judgment again.

Pros and Cons Template

People often think of a pros and cons list as something mechanical. Two columns. Quick answers. A simple weighing of benefits and consequences. But a pros and cons list can become something deeper. A way to understand your emotional landscape. A way to separate fear from truth. A way to see options clearly when the mind feels crowded.

When you consider using this tool, pause and breathe first. Then begin by exploring the advantages. Not just the surface-level ones. Look for emotional benefits. Look for the ways the decision might support your values. Look for the ways it might help you grow.

Then explore the disadvantages. Again, go deeper than inconvenience. Look for emotional costs. Look for what the decision might take from your time, your relationships, your sense of peace. Look for any patterns from the past that might influence how you feel.

As you complete both sides, notice which feelings arise. Notice where your body tightens or softens. Notice which thoughts feel expansive and which feel restrictive. The list is not meant to make the decision for you. It is meant to reveal the truth beneath your first reactions.

Marcus Aurelius taught that clarity comes when the mind examines things as they are, not as fear distorts them. The pros and cons reflection helps you do exactly that.

The Advice Filter Checklist

In a world full of voices, choosing which ones to trust becomes an essential skill. Many people offer advice. Some from love. Some from fear. Some from their own unresolved history. Some because they believe their way is the only way. Not all advice deserves equal weight.

This checklist is a reflective guide, not a set of rigid rules. When someone offers you advice, move through these questions slowly.

Ask yourself if the person understands your situation fully. Not just the surface, but the context beneath it.

Ask yourself if this person has made wise decisions in their own life, especially in the area they are advising you about.

Ask yourself whether their advice aligns with your values rather than their preferences.

Ask whether their words create calm or pressure.

Ask whether you feel expanded or diminished after speaking with them.

Also ask yourself if the person benefits from the decision they want you to make. There is nothing wrong with people having motives. But clarity requires recognizing them.

Finally, ask yourself whether your body relaxes or tightens when you consider following their guidance. The body often tells the truth before the mind does.

Lao Tzu said, **"He who knows others is learned. He who knows himself is wise."** When you filter advice through self-awareness, you strengthen your own wisdom.

The Goal Mapping Grid

People often imagine goals as distant destinations. Something to reach far in the future. Something large. Something intimidating. But goals are not destinations. They are directions. They pull you toward a life that feels more aligned, more grounded, more meaningful.

The Goal Mapping Grid is not a chart or table. It is a way of thinking. A way of breaking something overwhelming into manageable pieces.

Begin with the intention. What do you want? Not the polished answer you might give others. The honest one you whisper to yourself. Once you have that intention, consider the emotional reason behind it. Why does this matter to you? What part of your life would change if this goal were reached?

Next, identify the barriers. Be honest. Fear. Time. Money. Energy. Old habits. Lack of confidence. Naming barriers does not weaken you. It strengthens you because you see clearly what stands in your path.

Then consider one or two small actions that move you closer to the intention. Not grand steps. Not dramatic transformation. Something simple. Something human. Something you can do this week. Goals become real through small, repeated actions.

Thoreau once said, **"Success usually comes to those who are too busy to be looking for it."** Meaning that progress grows from movement, not obsession with outcomes.

When you use the Goal Mapping Grid mindset, your life stops feeling like a distant plan and starts feeling like a series of small choices leading toward something honest.

Daily Decision Journal

Your mind makes hundreds of decisions each day. Many pass unnoticed. But certain decisions carry emotional weight. They influence your relationships. Your work. Your health. Your sense of identity. The Daily Decision Journal helps you slow down enough to see these moments clearly. You do not need to write long entries. One or two sentences may be enough.

Begin by noticing one decision each day that felt important. A decision to speak up. Or stay quiet. A decision to rest. Or keep going. A decision to spend. Or save. A decision to set a boundary. A decision to connect with someone. A decision to let something go.

Write what the decision was. Write how it made you feel. Write what influenced your choice. Fatigue. Fear. Hope. Love. Habit. Intuition. Write whether you felt aligned with the decision afterward.

Over time, patterns will appear. You will see where your strengths live. You will see where certain emotions influence you more than you realized. You will see where you avoid certain choices. You will see where clarity rises naturally. These patterns will guide your future decisions more reliably than any outside advice.

Santiago Dagon wrote, **"A life becomes clear when a person becomes curious about their own choices."** Curiosity opens space. Space opens clarity. Clarity opens new paths.

The Daily Decision Journal is not a tool for perfection. It is a tool for presence. It helps you become aware of the person you are becoming one decision at a time.

These tools are simple, but they carry depth. They encourage reflection. They strengthen self-trust. They guide you gently back to your own wisdom.

Use them in difficult times. Use them in ordinary moments. Use them whenever you feel pulled in too many directions.

Each tool brings you closer to the same truth. You are capable of choosing well when you choose with awareness.

APPENDIX B

CASE STUDIES

Real People, Real Decisions, Real Outcomes.

These case studies come from the patterns I have witnessed over many years. The stories are not tied to any single individual. They are composites, formed from real themes, real struggles, and real turning points. Each reflects how ordinary people make decisions in difficult circumstances, and how those decisions shape the next chapter of their lives.

Santiago Dagon once wrote, **"A life changes one honest moment at a time."** These stories reveal those honest moments. Quiet ones. Tender ones. Painful ones. Transformative ones.

Case Study 1 - The Promotion That Felt Wrong

Elena worked in a fast-paced marketing department. She was talented, respected, and admired for her creative work. When a management position opened, her supervisors encouraged her to apply. The promotion promised a higher salary and prestige. On paper, it made sense. Everyone around her celebrated the possibility.

But something felt off.

Elena felt a heaviness in her stomach every time she imagined taking the role. She enjoyed creating, not supervising. She feared losing the part of her job that brought joy. Yet she worried others would judge her if she declined.

She sat with her decision for several weeks. She wrote in her decision journal. She noticed that every time she imagined saying Yes, her body tensed. And every time she imagined staying in her current role, she breathed more easily.

She declined the promotion.

There was surprise. Some quiet judgment. But six months later, she was happier than ever. She had kept what she genuinely loved. She had honored herself.

Outcome: Choosing alignment over expectation brought long-term fulfillment. Elena discovered that success is not always upward. Sometimes it is inward.

Case Study 2 - Staying Married for The Children

Daniel and Maria were together for fifteen years. They loved their children deeply. They shared history, home, and responsibilities. But the marriage had slowly eroded. Communication had become strained. Resentment grew quietly between them. They stayed because they believed staying was best for the children.

Years passed. The house became quieter. The tension became heavier. Their children began to sense the emotional distance between their parents.

One night, their oldest child asked, "Why do you both look sad all the time?" That question held a mirror to the truth.

They entered marriage counseling. Not to repair the marriage at first, but to understand it. Counseling revealed that staying together out of obligation was harming the family more than helping. Eventually, they made the difficult decision to divorce with compassion rather than hostility.

It was painful. But it was honest.

A year later, their children said, "You both seem happier now." The home became calmer. Co-parenting became an act of respect rather than conflict.

Outcome: Leaving the marriage with intentional kindness created a healthier environment for everyone. The decision was painful, but healing.

Case Study 3 - The Burnout That Led to A Second Chance

Sofia had been in hospital nursing for twelve years. She cared deeply about patients, but the emotional and physical demands had become overwhelming. Long shifts. Sleepless nights. Constant emergencies. Over time, she noticed numbness. She no longer felt joy in her work. She felt exhausted even after resting.

She feared quitting. Nursing was all she had ever known. She feared disappointing her family. She feared financial instability. But burnout was affecting her health.

One day she fainted at work. Her body finally spoke the truth she had ignored.

During leave, Sofia reflected on her life. She realized she still loved caring for others, but not in that environment. She began exploring community health work and eventually transitioned into a role focused on patient education and support. Fewer emergencies. More meaningful conversations. A schedule that allowed breathing room.

She rediscovered purpose.

Outcome: Burnout became the turning point. Changing roles saved her health and renewed her calling.

Case Study 4 - The Financial Decision Made from Fear

Michael grew up in a home with financial instability. As an adult, he saved obsessively. He avoided risks. He never spent money on anything unnecessary. He believed this discipline protected him.

When a close friend invited him to join a small business venture, Michael wanted to say Yes. The idea inspired him. But fear told him that any risk was dangerous. He declined.

Years later he realized he had avoided opportunities not because they were wrong, but because old fear controlled him. He entered life coaching and slowly learned to separate his childhood experiences from his adult abilities.

Eventually he invested modestly in a different venture, one that aligned with his skills. It did well. Not because it guaranteed success, but because he chose it consciously rather than reactively.

Outcome: Michael learned that fear-driven decisions keep life small. Awareness allowed him to choose with confidence rather than anxiety.

Case Study 5 - The Digital Life That Replaced Real Life

Jasmine spent hours each day on her phone. She followed influencers, news updates, and lifestyle trends. She compared herself endlessly to others. She believed she was failing because her life did not look like what she saw online.

Her relationships weakened. Her sleep suffered. Her self-worth declined.

One night, she realized she had spent an entire evening scrolling without speaking to her partner who was sitting beside her. She saw the loneliness in his eyes. That moment broke something open in her.

She began taking small steps. Removing notifications. Leaving her phone in another room during meals. Going outside alone each morning without technology.

Within months, she felt clearer. Calmer. More connected. Her relationship strengthened. She regained parts of herself she had forgotten.

Outcome: Reducing digital overwhelm restored her mental health and revived her connection with the real world.

Case Study 6 - A Child Lost in The Noise

Anthony and Marisa noticed their teenage son was becoming withdrawn. He spent hours gaming. He struggled in school. He snapped easily. They assumed it was typical teenage behavior until a teacher called and expressed concern.

They sat down with him one evening. He broke down. He admitted he felt overwhelmed by school, social pressure, and expectations. He felt he could not talk to anyone because everyone was always busy or distracted.

That conversation changed the family dynamic. They began practicing family dinners without devices. They created space for weekly check-ins. They listened without correcting. They helped him find a therapist. Slowly, he began to feel seen.

Outcome: Awareness and intentional connection helped him recover emotionally. Presence became the tool that healed the family.

Case Study 7 - Caring for An Aging Parent

Lydia lived three states away from her mother. When her mother's health declined, Lydia felt torn. Her job required her.

Her children needed her. Yet she felt a deep responsibility to help.

For months she carried guilt. She believed she was failing someone no matter what she did. Eventually, she realized she needed support. She spoke with siblings. She spoke with neighbors. She spoke with professionals. Together, they created a care plan.

Her mother received help. Lydia received relief. And the family found a rhythm.

Outcome: Asking for support reduced guilt and created sustainable care for her mother and stability for her own life.

Case Study 8 - When A Dream Changes

Ethan had wanted to become a musician since childhood. He pursued it for years. But the industry drained him. He struggled financially. He felt disconnected from the joy he once had.

Letting go felt like failure. But holding on felt like drowning.

After many months of reflection, he chose a new direction. He began teaching music instead of performing. He found fulfillment in helping others discover the joy he once felt. His dream had not died. It had transformed.

Outcome: He learned that dreams are allowed to evolve. Purpose adapts as life does.

Case Study 9 - The Friendship That Needed Boundaries

Rachel had a friend she loved deeply, but the friendship had become emotionally draining. Her friend relied on her constantly for support yet offered little in return. Rachel feared setting boundaries. She feared losing the relationship.

Over time, the exhaustion became heavier than the fear.

Rachel finally expressed her limits. Calmly. Compassionately. Her friend reacted with surprise, then anger. Weeks passed. Then months. Eventually, her friend returned with a softer heart. The relationship became healthier.

And if it had not, Rachel would have been at peace knowing she chose her well-being with honesty.

Outcome: Setting boundaries saved the friendship and restored Rachel's emotional balance.

Case Study 10 - Choosing Love Again After Heartbreak

Aisha had experienced a painful breakup that left her feeling unworthy of love. She told herself she would never trust again. She avoided dating. She avoided intimacy. She avoided vulnerability.

Years later she met someone kind. Patient. Respectful. But fear resurfaced. She wanted to run. She wanted to protect herself from the possibility of pain.

She began therapy. Slowly, she learned that vulnerability is not a weakness. She learned that she did not need to be perfect to be loved. She learned that new relationships do not repeat old wounds when awareness has grown.

She chose to open her heart again. Carefully. Gradually. With intention.

Outcome: Healing allowed her to experience love in a healthier and more authentic way.

Santiago Dagon writes, **"Human lives change through small truths spoken at the right time."** These case studies reflect those truths. They show that decisions rarely unfold cleanly. They show that courage appears quietly. They show that growth emerges through awareness, not perfection.

Use these stories as mirrors. Use them as gentle reminders that you are not alone in your struggles. Others have walked similar paths. Others have chosen with fear and still found clarity. Others have fallen and stood again. You will too.

ABOUT AUTHOR

Nicholas J. Matyas is an American writer, educator, and personal development consultant whose work bridges reflection, faith, and the quiet search for meaning. His writing explores the meeting place between the seen and unseen, the ordinary and the eternal. Through his stories, he invites readers to pause, to listen, and to remember the sacred in everyday life.

Santiago Dagon is the contemplative voice and pen name through which Nicholas J. Matyas gives form to the deeper questions of the heart. Writing as Dagon allows him to step beyond the limits of a single perspective and speak from the timeless space between history and spirit. The name has come to represent not just an author, but a philosophy that wisdom is born from stillness, and that compassion is the truest form of understanding.

Together, Nicholas J. Matyas and Santiago Dagon write as one voice blending the human and the mystical, the factual and the poetic, to tell stories that remind us of who we are and what we carry within us.

ABOUT DISCOVERY WALKABOUT PRESS

Discovery Walkabout Press was founded on a simple belief: that reflection is not withdrawal from life, but a deeper way of living it. Its mission is to create media that nurture awareness, emotional intelligence, and intergenerational understanding. Media, in the form of books, articles, reflective guides, modern parables, contemplative workbooks and seminars that help readers rediscover peace, purpose, curiosity and live more consciously, love more gently, and see the extraordinary within the ordinary within themselves and the world around them.

Each title published under Discovery Walkabout Press follows a quiet philosophy: learning begins in stillness, wisdom grows through connection, and creativity flourishes when the mind is calm. The Press supports projects that bridge the spiritual and the practical, inviting readers to walk slowly through their own questions rather than rush toward answers.

At its heart, Discovery Walkabout Press stands for mindful storytelling, a journey of self-discovery, compassion, and clarity across generations.

As a publishing house and creative development studio we invite new and existing authors to grow together with us. Please reach out and contact us.

To follow our ongoing works, visit Discovery Walkabout Press https://discoverywalkabout.com

"We do not find truth by running faster. We find it by learning how to walk with wonder." - *Santiago Dagon*

www.ingramcontent.com/pod-product-compliance
Lightning Source LLC
LaVergne TN
LVHW010838120826
845149LV00017B/3275